SEO for
Google 2021

All the Secret Search Engine Optimization (SEO)
Tips that Google Doesn't Want You to Know

Ricardo Carreras Lario

SEO for Google 2021
© Iberanálisis SL, 2020.
© All rights of this edition are reserved in favour of Editorial Iberanálisis.

First edition: septembre 2021
ISBN: 9798684304231

Editorial Iberanálisis SL
Paseo de la Castellana 143, Planta 10
Madrid 28046
http://www.t-position.com/

Layout and design: Paulo Rosas Arce and Lucía Lasprilla
Impreso en España - Printed in Spain

To the collaborators of the marketing and digital communication consulting firm, Top Position, professionals in search engine positioning, devoted followers of Google, dedicated to the good practices of white SEO.

To the students and alumni of the (official) Master's Degree in Digital Marketing, Communication and Social Networks, of the Universidad Camilo José Cela, and ID Digital School. They are masters of the new trades and digital arts.

About the Author

RICARDO CARRERAS LARIO has a PhD from the University Complutense de Madrid. His doctoral thesis (cum laude) analyzed how Google works. In 2008 he founded the Top Position Digital Marketing Consultancy, which specialises in search engine positioning  and digital reputation, and which he has chaired ever since. In 2012 he wrote his first book about Google, entitled "Toreando a Google". Since 2014, he has been Director of the University Master's Degree in Digital Marketing, Communication and Social Networks (UCJC), the only official face-to-face or semi-face-to-face Master's Degree that can be studied in Madrid in this discipline. Carreras is also Member of The Board of Directors at Carreras Grupo Logístico, a leading company in Spain in integrated logistics services -transport, warehousing, distribution, pallet racking and co-packing - and participates in other companies.

He has studied and lived in 6 countries, besides Spain, and speaks fluent English, French and German.

His Twitter account is Riccarreras
https://twitter.com/riccarreras
and his linkedin account is
https://www.linkedin.com/in/ricardo-carreras lario-781522/

Content

Introduction

"SEO for Google 2021" is the sequel to my first book about the search engine, "Toreando a Google".

The first one explained what the most relevant factors are for a web page to get the first position in Google results.

This second one has a more practical approach than the first one, and explains what you, the reader, have to do, to succeed in Google, through clear and concise advice.

If in the first one I analyzed which are the criteria or factors that cause a web page -among the thousands or millions of candidates- to appear in the first positions of the list of the first page of Google search results -called SERP -search engine result pages-, in this one I will focus more on questions and practical advice, which will help you, reader, to achieve results in Google.

Internet and digital communication

There is no need to write much about the importance of the Internet and search engines in particular. They are part of our lives. We couldn't live without them anymore.

Just to point out that this importance keeps growing, it has not yet reached its full development. They are, therefore, more relevant every day.

Some interesting facts:
- Google has more than 90% of the world market share, in some countries like Spain, it exceeds 95%.
- It receives more than 60,000 searches per second.
- It had a capitalization of 826 billion at the end of 2019.
- On average, an Internet user performs four searches a day.
- Globally, investment in digital advertising is already superceeding 40%. It is expected to exceed 50% by 2021. Of that vast repository Google takes more than half.

What is a Search Engine?

Expert Jerri Ledford explains in her book SEO: Search Engine Optimization Bible (2008) that a search engine is "a program that uses applications that collect information from Web pages and then indexes and stores that information in a database.

The experts Susan Esparza and Bruce Clay, for their part, specify, in their work Search Engine Optimization (2009), the following: "A search engine is an application designed to search for specific keywords and then group the results by their relevance. [...] Search engines such as Google, Yahoo and Microsoft Live were created to dispense with intermediaries and bring your users directly to you without hindrance or difficulty".

From this we can conclude that Search engines are programs that allow Internet users to quickly find relevant information on specific keywords.

Chapter 1
Short history of search engines

Search engines have been associated with the Internet since the very beginning of the Network of Networks.

According to a study[1] by Leiden University (Netherlands) and other authors, the first search engine worthy of the name was called Archie[2] , short for Archives. It was created by Alan Emtage, a computer science student at McGill University (Montreal, Canada) in 1990. This first search engine indexed file names, creating an open database that gave as a result of the search the files that matched the search word.

In 1991 Gopher[3] was born, created by Mark McCahill at the University of Minnesota, a protocol that allowed the appearance of two new search programs: Veronica and Jughead. Like Archie, these early engines searched for file names hosted in Gopher's index systems. As a point of interest, although Archie was not related to the homonymous comic book series, these two new engines took names of characters from the series, thus linking with Archie.

On September 2, 1993 came what can be considered as the first search engine: W3Catalog[4] . A few months before, in June of the same year, the first spider or crawler robot had seen the light -web crawler- in English- that went all over the Web, then processing the different existing web pages. The robot, named the "Wanderer of the Global Web" -World Wide Web Wanderer-

---

[1] http://www.leidenuniv.nl/letteren/internethistory/index.php3-m=6&c=7.htm#se
[2] http://en.wikipedia.org/wiki/Archie_search_engine
[3] http://en.wikipedia.org/wiki/Gopher_%28protocol%29
[4] http://en.wikipedia.org/wiki/W3Catalog

finished its work in 1995. It took two years to track the entire Web. The index it produced was called Wandex. Its author was Matthew Gray of MIT -Massachusetts Institute of Technology.

The second search engine, Aliweb, was launched in November 1993. And a month later, JumpStation was born. This search engine, which appeared in December 1993, already has the basic features of today's search engines. Indeed, despite its limited capacity, JumpStation processed only the titles of web pages and their main headings to build its index; it did so by using a robot to capture the information, offering results based on keywords and presenting those results in lists of web addresses that matched the word being searched for. In other words, it already looked remarkably like today's Google.

It began indexing on December 12, 1993. It was hosted by the University of Stirling (Scotland, United Kingdom). Its author, Jonathon Fletcher, had recently graduated from the same university. He was responsible for its launch and subsequent management, but the project failed due to lack of resources. He left the University of Stirling at the end of 1994 without having secured funding from that university. By then the engine had over 270,000 indexed web pages.

Adam Wishart and Regula Bochsler tell in their book - Leaving Reality Behind: etoys v eToys.com, and other battles to control cyberspace, Ecco, 2003 - these and other details of the history of JumpStation and the avatars of its founder.

We continue to move forward and a few months later, on April 20, 1994, we find Webcrawler, the first full text search engine, that is, it crawled and indexed all the words in a web page and not just the main ones. The Webcrawler page still exists. It is http://www.webcrawler.com/. It no longer offers the original search engine, but a mixture of results from today's major search engines - Google, Yahoo, Bing.

Lycos (http://www.lycos.com/) was another search engine born in 1994, with a great commercial drive. The company grew until it was bought by Terra[5] , the Telefónica subsidiary in the middle of the Internet bubble in 2000, for the not insignificant sum of 2 trillion of the old pesetas or 12.5 billion dollars. Four years later, in 2004, it was sold - for a fraction of that amount.

Let's go back to the search engines. Shortly after the appearance of Webcrawer and Lycos, new search engines proliferated such as Magullan, Infoseek, Excite, Inktomi, Northern Light, AltaVista and Yahoo. At that time, their use was already beginning to spread in the United States.

In 1996, the company of the famous browser Netscape wanted to reach an exclusive agreement with a single search engine that would appear by default in its program. In the end, five of them, Yahoo, Magellan, Lycos, Infoseek, and Excite, reached a curious agreement and paid five million dollars a year per head to rotate the browser's search engine page. This gives an idea of the importance that search engines started having already at that early date. It is not surprising to learn that several of the companies that launched search engines at that time "caught their fingers" in the madness of the Internet bubble, especially between 1999 and 2001.

By then, a search engine born in 1998 was beginning to stand out: Google. Its search results were better than the others, and through word of mouth, it was gaining ground.

Microsoft, on the other hand, launched its search engine - MSN Search - in 1998, using the Inktomi engine as a base. Six years later, Microsoft began the transition to its own search engine, which uses its own robot -msnbot-, relaunched strongly in 2009 under the name of Bing.

---

[5] http://www.elmundo.es/navegante/2000/05/17/terra_lycos.html

Despite fierce competition, Google's global desktop market share in 2019 is 75.74%, according to the prestigious <u>Netmarketshare</u>[6] measurement. The figure for mobiles and tablets is even higher.

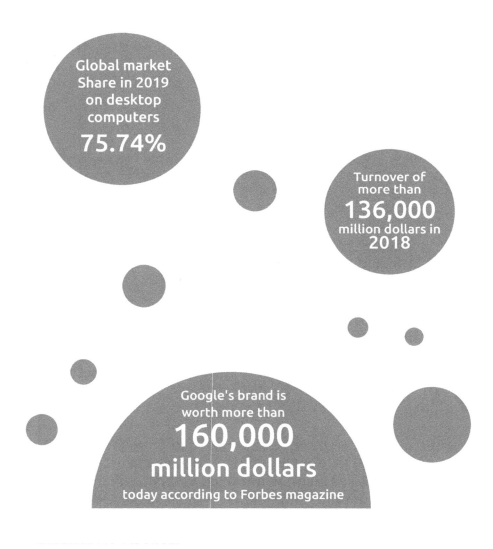

Global market Share in 2019 on desktop computers
75.74%

Turnover of more than
136,000
million dollars in **2018**

Google's brand is worth more than
160,000 million dollars
today according to Forbes magazine

---

[6] https://netmarketshare.com/

Chapter 2
Brief history of Google

The search engine and the company that launched it represent one of the most striking success stories of our time.

Google was originally a research project by Larry Page and Sergei Brin, two brilliant PhD students at Stanford University (USA). Page came up with the idea of investigating the mathematical characteristics of the world-wide web -www. To do this, he wanted to analyze and understand the structure of the links between the different web pages.

His tutor, Ferry Winograd, had encouraged him to choose that topic. Page set out to investigate which web pages link to another page, thinking that the number and nature of those links was very valuable information - regarding the linked page. He was thinking about the role of academic citations, which are very important in the university world and particularly in the United States. Page called that initial project "BackRub. His friend Sergei Brin, a secular Jewish doctoral student -like Page- of Russian origin, immediately joined the project. Page's tracker began to travel the Internet in March 1996. It was based on Page's own Stanford University website. To crystallize the data that the crawler collected about the links to each page, the two developed the PageRank algorithm.

When analyzing the results of BackRub - which consisted of a list of links to a specific page, classified by importance - they thought that a search engine that took into account these criteria would produce better search results than the search engines existing at that time - which only analyzed factors internal to a web page, such as the number of times a keyword was repeated. Thus was created the first seed of the new search engine, called Rankdex.

The initial search engine used the Stanford website, with the domain google.stanford.edu.

They registered the domain Google on September 15, 1997. The firm Google, Inc. was born on September 4, 1998 in a friend's garage in Menlo Park, California.

Andy Bechtolsheim - Andreas von Bechtolsheim - a German-American entrepreneur who had co-founded Sun Microsystems a few years earlier in 1982, provided the initial "seed" capital for Google. His $100,000 check, handed over in August 1998, would be the best investment of his life.

Later, in June 1999, two venture capital firms, Sequioa Capital and Kleiner Perkins Caufield & Byers, invested in the company with a capital contribution of $25 million.

Initially, the two founders Brin and Page were opposed to placing advertising on their search engine. They would soon change their minds. Years later, under pressure from investors to make profits, Google copied the system invented by Overture -a firm later bought by Yahoo- of contextual advertising, based on the keywords searched, which is now known as Adwords. Yahoo sued them for it and Google had to pay a considerable amount -although not disclosed- of money for Yahoo to abandon the legal proceedings.

The name "Google" is an alteration of the word "googol," which means the number represented by 1 to 100. Enid Blyton had already used the word decades earlier, in the ninth chapter of her book The Magic Faraway Tree, entitled Google Bun.

This is what Google's homepage looked like in September 1998

By the end of 1998, Google had already indexed 60 million pages.

The company was established in March 1999 in Palo Alto, in Silicon Valley. After moving twice more due to its rapid growth, Google rented office space at its current location in Mountain View - 1600 Amphitheatre Parkway. They are still there - they bought the building from their landlords in 2006 for $319 million. Their offices are called the Googleplex - from Google Complex.

Google's motto has always been "do not be evil", as opposed to Microsoft, a giant that had a reputation for being unscrupulous. However, we have already seen that from its beginnings the firm also began to deviate from impeccable conduct in some matters that affected its profitability.

Google was first listed on the stock exchange on 19 August 2004. The operation was a great success and the almost twenty million shares rose by twenty percent on the same day. The starting price was $85 per share. Within a few hours, they were worth more than 100 dollars. Today they are worth twenty times as much. The firm is part of the NASDAQ technology index, and the S&P index, with the GOOG symbol.

Google's success in the search engine market, as we have already indicated, has been spectacular. Its simple interface (which resembles Altavista's at the outset), together with the quality of its search results, explains market rates of between 66% and 95% in all Western culture countries. That quality is based on its refined algorithm, which outperforms all others to date. We can talk about the fact that Google launched the second version of the search engine, as the expert Javier Casares says in his SEO guide. This second version, now imitated by Google's main competitors, consists of taking into account external factors, a website's environment - especially the number and quality of links to it - and not just internal factors as others have done up to now.

> Having dominated the search industry, the successful company has expanded into a large number of economic sectors beyond the initial business. It has launched its own e-mail service - gmail - mobile phones, its own browser to compete with Window - Chrome - and acquired major companies such as YouTube, bought for $1.65 billion on October 9, 2006, or DoubleClick, an Internet advertising company acquired in April 2007 for $3.1 billion.
>
> Today the verb Google is incorporated into English. Since 2006 it has been included in the Oxford English Dictionary, the equivalent of the dictionary of the Royal Spanish Academy of Language.
>
> The Google brand is worth more than 160 billion dollars today, according to Forbes magazine.
>
> Google had a turnover of more than 136 billion dollars in 2018.

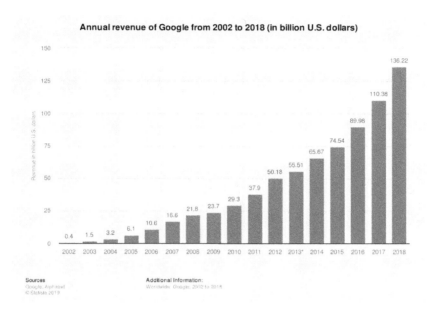

Annual revenue of Google from 2002 to 2018 (in billion U.S. dollars)

Google's annual turnover from 2002 to 2018
(In billions of dollars)

And it has just over 103,000 employees. That means , each of them has a turnover of more than a million dollars - exactly 1,320,000 dollars. This places Google in the top ten technology companies that generate the most revenue per employee.

These incredible figures can only be understood if we look at another fundamental fact that has not received enough media interest, and which explains how Google can turn over more than a million dollars per employee and earn with each of them more than four times the average of large companies: Google has many more computers than employees. In other words, it is an automated processing company that is primarily run by robots - computers that have been properly upgraded by the company's engineers. It is also curious to note that Google does not clearly publish the number of computers it owns, but estimates range from 300,000 to six million. In any case, we are talking about an enormous number of computers - robots. They are, to a large extent, Google's strength, and they explain its success.

In parallel with its impressive rise in recent years, Google has carried out a series of questionable activities, or activities of dubious morality, which have earned it a series of very different and varied criticisms - from criticism of the lack of privacy of some of its products, to reproaches about its complicity with the Chinese government.

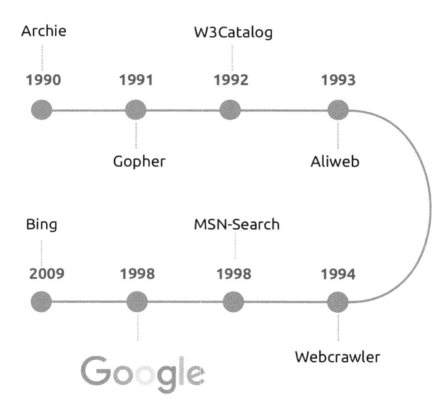

Chapter 3
How Google works at its core

Let's try to explain how Google performs the feat of processing and analyzing the entire network. The process of searching in Google is as follows:

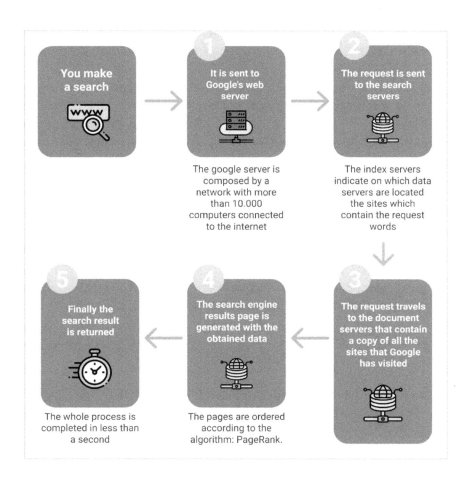

After a search, Google generates SERP, Search Engine Result Pages, through its complex and secret mathematical algorithm that takes into account more than two hundred factors.

According to expert Ledford: "When the user performs a search for a word or a phrase, an algorithm examines the information stored in the database and returns a list of links to web pages that appear to match the user's search term.

It should be remembered that Google is a text-based search engine, not a semantic one - as perhaps those of the future will be - and therefore does not understand what its results reflect.

On the other hand, everything indicates that the result of a Google search is mostly a combination of two classifications. On the one hand, there is the popularity index which, as we will see in depth below, corresponds to PageRank, a unique mathematical value calculated in a complex way and updated frequently. In this way, through the PageRank, Google classifies all the web pages it has indexed - billions - in a list, according to the PageRank points they have. As indicated by Amy Langville and Carl D. Meyer in their work "PageRank and beyond, the science of search engine rankings" (2006), this classification, defined by the amount of PageRank, is independent of the specific search - in English, "query-independent". It is obtained through a complex analysis of the link structure of the entire Internet.

The other essential part of the final ranking is an index of content, which is dependent on the individual search.

Google performs a ranking for each keyword, which contains the list of all relevant web pages for that search and a score for each one, given by a large number of factors. This ranking, in turn, is combined with PageRank to achieve the final ranking.

Chapter 4
Some concepts

To understand what follows, it is helpful to master the following concepts:

Title tag: tag used to define the name of a web page. To obtain the results of this factor, different tools can be used, such as Quake SEO in different browsers.

Length of text: refers to the total number of words contained in the body of a web page. It can be seen for free with Quake SEO.

Keyword density (PC) in the main text of the page: Is the number (in percentage) of times the keyword is repeated within the main text of the web page. It can be seen for free with Quake SEO.

PageRank (PR): registered trademark by Google. It consists of a complex mathematical formula that gives each web page a numerical value -represented from 0 to 10-, depending on its importance. As we will see later, the real value of PageRank is not linear, but exponential, and therefore the values of the scale 0 to 10 are misleading, since the distance between each number is a factor 8 -the 2 is 8 times more powerful than the 1. Google no longer publishes the PageRank values of a web page, and it cannot be known exactly, although there are very similar indicators that can be used.

Number of external inbound links: This is the number of hyperlinks (links) a web page receives from other web pages on the Internet.

Number of links to the entire Web site: This criterion takes into account the links that the entire Web site - main page and all internal pages - receives from other Internet pages.

Number of outgoing links: this refers to the total sum of external web pages that link from the same web page.

Number of internal links: This refers to the total sum of links to internal pages or sections that are linked from the same web page. Can be viewed for free with Quake SEO.

Age of the website: This criterion takes into account the age -in years- of the website where the first page is hosted. It can be viewed for free with Quake SEO.

Keyword in domain name: this factor takes into account whether or not the main domain of the website where the web page is hosted in first position has the keyword in question.

Keyword in URL of the page: in the same way as the previous criterion, it takes into account whether the keyword is contained in any part of the URL of the page analyzed. For example, the Wikipedia page that talks about the "car" contains that word in its url:
https://en.wikipedia.org/wiki/Car.

Number of bars in the URL: this is the number of bars (symbol: /) that a web page contains in its URL.

Number of pages indexed in Google for the whole site: this is the number of pages of a website that has Google indexed in its index. This value can be obtained through Google itself, by writing site:domain.com in the search engine.

Keyword in H1 header: H1 header texts are those written between the <h1>...</h1> tags in the HTML code of a Web page.

Keyword in H2 header: the texts H2 header, are the texts written between <h2>...</h2> tags, in the HTML code of a Web page.

Keyword in ALT tags: The <alt> attribute defines an alternative text for images and other elements of a page when the user uses a text browser.

Keyword usage (density) in ALT tags: The <alt> attribute defines an alternative text for images and other elements of a page when the user uses a text browser. For this factor the number of times (in percentage) that the keyword is repeated in the ALT tag of the analyzed web page is counted.

Use (density) of keyword in internal link anchor text: This criterion refers to the link texts of the hyperlinks pointing to a Web page in the same domain. The number of times (in percentage) that the keyword is repeated in the internal link anchor texts is calculated.

Use (density) of keyword in outbound link anchor texts: This criterion refers to the link texts of the hyperlinks pointing to a web page outside the analysed domain. The number of times (in percentage) that the keyword is repeated in the outbound link anchor texts is calculated.

Keyword usage (density) in internal link URLs: This criterion refers to link URLs pointing to a web page from the same domain. The number of times (in percentage) the keyword is repeated in internal link URLs is calculated.

Keyword usage (density) in outbound link URLs: This criterion refers to link URLs that point to a web page outside the analyzed domain. The number of times (in percentage) that the keyword is repeated in outbound link URLs is calculated.

Keyword usage (density) in the description tag: the description tag is used to describe what a web page contains. This factor analyzes the number of times (in percentage) that the keyword is repeated in the description text of the analyzed web page.

Keyword usage (density) in the keyword tag: The keyword tag allows you to define which terms are important for a web page. This criterion takes into account the number of times (in percentage) that the keyword is repeated in the keyword tag.

Keyword usage (density) in the first sentence of the main text: The first sentence of the main text is found after the <body> tag in the HTML code of a web page. This factor looks at the number of times (in percentage) the keyword is repeated in the first sentence of the main text.

Chapter 5
Strategy

Before detailing what the most important factors are for getting good results on Google, and how to manage them, some strategic issues need to be addressed.

The first thing we need to know is what we want to achieve.

What traffic do we want to attract? What is the objective? Is it to sell gym equipment over the Internet? Do we want to influence the political debate on a specific issue? Or are we an NGO that wants people to support a specific cause? How will our audience find our website? How can we convince them to buy what we sell?

Are we looking for informed visitors? Do we want to sell a product?

Once we know what we want, the next step is to define our keyword strategy.

The Google universe is fragmented into keywords. The results page for "travel offers to Indonesia" is nothing like the one that shows the answer to the search "Donald Trump policy proposals" or "how to cook a sea bream in salt". The goals of the user searching for one or the other are very different.

It is necessary to analyse which are the keywords that - alone or in combination - we need to achieve our goals.

it would be prudent to study which of them we should compete for, since it would not be efficient to try to stand out in all of them. And sometimes it will be almost impossible.

Finally, we will have to study how the combinations of keywords we choose fit into our website -or into several of them. That is, how they develop and relate to each other.

If we launch an online business, for example, a store that sells boxes of wine directly to consumers, we must analyze who our potential customers are and how they behave. Also who are the competitors that dominate the market and what are they offering. A study of consumers, the market and the competition should therefore precede any online initiative.

Going back to the keyword combinations, there are three fundamental questions:

1) Which ones are our customers or potential users looking for?
2) Which ones do our competitors use?
3) How are we going to organize and deploy them on our website?

It is very important to know the answers to these questions.

The first objective is usually to appear first - or one of the first - for the name of our company or business. This should be the easy part of the job. We can achieve much more.

Likewise, it is not very helpful to get top positions for keyword combinations that are important to us, but that no one is looking for. Someone for example wants to appear in Google for the search "dentist registered in Madrid". We can easily achieve that, but how many consumers are looking for it? It is better to stand out for the search "dentist in Madrid". Basically because many more people are looking for that combination.

On the other hand, if we want to get good results for generic keywords (dentists, travel, plants), we face a huge challenge. The level of competition is already brutal for practically any word, so it is very difficult to achieve. And besides, the vast majority of people - 75% according to some studies - search for combinations of two, three or more words, while only a small minority carry out single-word searches.

Many more people search for "dentist in Madrid -or in another specific city- than for "dentist". And those people want something concrete - a dentist in their city - while the person looking for "dentist" may be a student looking for a definition or a child looking for what that word means.

This is the concept of "long tail". People look for, for example, trips to a specific place, rather than the word "trip" in general.

The general marketing concept is developed by Chris Anderson in his book "the long tail".

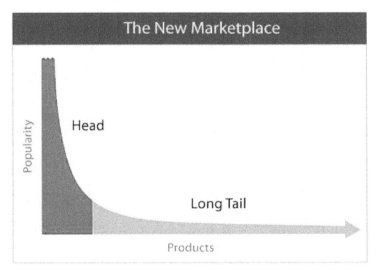

The graph above shows the philosophy behind a "long tail" strategy. Applied to Google, this means that there are many searches for specific products, for example "second-hand treadmills" or "cheap dentists in Valladolid". This is the basis for the success of, for example, amazon.com

The ideal is to find many combinations of various keywords that people are looking for, but that the competition has not yet saturated.

You should also avoid the temptation to fill the web pages of our site with text that is unreadable to the human eye, by repeating and rephrasing a particular keyword - keyword stuffing. A practice that is also penalised by Google, as we will see later on.

In short, you have to think about potential users, put yourself in their shoes, and use their language.

And then, how do you know what people are looking for?

We have a tool provided by Google itself. It is their keyword planning tool.[7]

In fact, this tool -which also has its deficiencies - is designed to help Google's customers when they buy its advertising. However, it can also be used to find out how many searches have one or more specific keyword.

It needs to be considered that the tool is not very precise, and must be used from Google Adwords.

Another free tool is Google Trends (https://trends.google.com/), also from Google, as the nameimplies . It allows you to know -again, in a somewhat inaccurate way- the searches for a keyword. It allows you to analyze it by country, time period, category and type of search.

If, for example, we search for "Google book", it tells us that in USA there are around 99 searches per week for this term.

---

[7] https://ads.google.com/intl/es_ES/home/

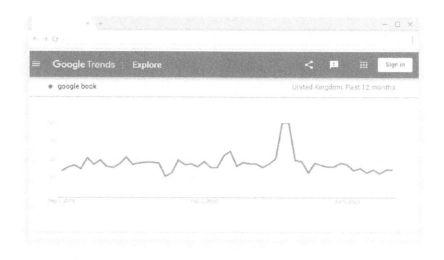

Search "google book", in google trends

If we search "dentists New York ", it gives us 56 searches, while "dental clinic New York" gives us 37.

Interestingly this tool allows us to know which were the most searched terms in 2018 in the USA.

Can you guess them? The number one is World Cup, followed by Hurricane Florence and Mac Miller, all according to Google.

In addition to these tools, there are some other paid tools to determine the number of searches. One of them is Semrush. com, which allows us to know which are the keywords in which a competitor stands out. Another, in English, is wordtracker, at http://www.wordtracker.com/

We can also ask the users we are interested in, what words they are looking for, informally, or professionally through market research tools such as surveys or focus groups.

Finally, Google also gives us suggestions for related words, both in the search box above and below the search results.

Once we know what the most common searches are, we'll need to analyze how competitive each one is.

The easiest way is to study how many web pages appear for the search operations for each of those keywords.

For example, going back to dentists, although dentists have more searches, they also have more competition.

If we search for "dentist new york" in Google, we see that there are about 82,200 results, while "dental clinic new york" has 18,900 results.

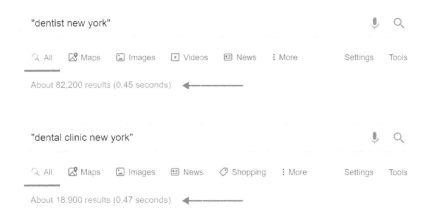

Number of results for each search

We must therefore calculate what the relationship is between the search volumes for each keyword combination, and the level of competence. A simple formula would be to divide for each keyword the estimated volume of searches by the number of web pages that contain it. And then we classify all the keywords according to that indicator. There are ways of fine tuning, for example, by analyzing which web pages contain a keyword and also receive links whose anchor text includes that keyword. To do this you have to search for allinanchor: keyword in Google. This will give us a smaller number of web pages. We will then have to calculate the ratio between the volume of searches and the web pages that receive links whose text contains that keyword. This will give us a more accurate indicator.

And we must also take into account which are qualitatively the results on the first page, because some will be more difficult to anticipate than others.

For example, if we search for a hotel in Ibiza, we will find the "usual suspects" in the first ten results, that is, huge websites that are very difficult to compete with, such as booking, expedia, trivago, etc. It will be almost impossible to beat these giants.

However, if we look for accommodation in Ibiza, or where to sleep in Ibiza, the outlook is more encouraging.

You should also establish some specific quantitative indicator on the first page of results, which will show us their difficulty. It can be as simple as adding up, for the first 10 results, on the one hand, the number of pages indexed in the whole website, the links that the website receives in general, all this multiplied by the age of the website and divided by 1000. This way we get an indicator of the structural strength of that page. We can add up the links that that particular page receives to get an approximate reference of the difficulty.

For the first result of a search, it would remain:

Difficulty Level= [Number of pages indexed in the whole website + number of links to the whole website] * age of the website/1000] + number of incoming links to the specific page.

Or more simply, we can use some of the tools that give us

indicators of the authority of a page and its domain. For example, the Semrush tool (semrush.com) gives us four types of indicators:

Page Score

Page Score measures the **number of links** pointing to a web page.

Domain Score

Domain Score measures the **number of links** pointing to a website as a whole.

Trust Score

Trust Score measures the reliability of a website or domain. It is calculated by analyzing t**he number of inbound links from pages with a high reputation. In other words, it is an indicator of the quality of the links a page or domain receives.**

Since the Trust Score analyses the most reliable links, if there is a big difference between Trust Score and Page Score of a page, it means that we are receiving a lot of low quality links.

Authority Score

Authority Score measures the overall strength of a domain. To calculate it SEMrush is based on:

- Link data, including Domain Score, Trust Score, and others
- Organic search data including organic traffic and positions
- Web traffic data

With any of these and other indicators we can analyze the level of difficulty of a first page of results for a given keyword.

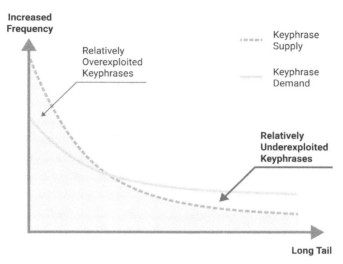

Keyword Market Analysis according to Popularity and Long Tail

We should take this into account to choose those that have the best relationship between search volume and competition.

Website structure

Once we choose the keywords for which we are going to compete, it is essential to choose how. Let me explain. The home page of our website should be reserved for the most difficult keywords, while other sections of our website should focus on secondary and tertiary searches.

For example, if we develop a site on travel to Japan, the home page should be optimized for those keywords, while other sections should aim at "cheap travel to Japan", "travel to Tokyo", etc. And we should use a blog for the long tail, i.e. publishing entries about trips to Naoshima in Japan, focused on those who want to visit that island.

Ideally, each web page within our website should be optimized for a single set of keywords. Although not ideal, we can optimize a web page for several groups of related keywords, but a single keyword or phrase must be optimized on a single web page on our site. Otherwise, we would enter a "cannibalization" of keywords that would weaken us before Google. This strategic principle is fundamental, although many forget it. That is, if I have a section that talks about traveling to Tokyo, I should not write a publication in my blog optimized for that search term. It is an inefficiency for users, and especially for Google, since we emit a dissonant signal.

Chapter 6
Indexing

Before we go on to analyse what the crucial factors are for obtaining good results on Google, we must explain, even in summary form, the subject of indexing on Google. In order to win a race, we must first register. If a web page is not indexed in Google, it is metaphysically impossible for it to achieve a good position in its search results. On the contrary, it will not appear in any results.

As we have already explained, Google has a series of automatic robots. The most famous of these is the so-called Googlebot. This is Google's main web crawler, also called a spider. Googlebot constantly crawls the Internet, discovering new pages and updated content from old pages, and adding them to the Google index.

Google uses a huge amount of computer equipment for this process of "digesting" billions of web pages. Googlebot uses an algorithmic crawling process: complex mathematical formulas determine which sites it has to crawl, how often it has to crawl, and how many web pages it has to search for on each site. This process starts with a list of webpage URLs generated from previous crawl processes and expands with data provided by webmasters. As Googlebot visits each of these websites, it detects links on their pages and adds them to the list of pages to crawl. New sites, changes to existing sites, and outdated links are detected and used to update the Google index. This means that Google has a 99% copy of the Internet stored in its "stomach" at all times - imagine the enormous amount of data that would be involved. This copy can be viewed for a month, even if the webpage is no longer available, in the "cache" function of the search results. There, Google shows us the last copy it has of a web page, as well as the time when Googlebot obtained the data.

Googlebot calculates how often it should go through a particular webpage, based on how little or how much that webpage is updated. If the webpage changes every few years, Googlebot will try to visit the webpage often, at the same frequency. If the website changes about once a month, Googlebot will visit it every 30 days. Webmasters can ask google to change this crawl frequency, within the Search Console tool (formerly called Webmaster Tools), at

http://support.google.com/webmasters/bin/answer.py?hl=en&answer=48620

You can see in detail the content of the official website of the Real Madrid in Google's cache. It reads that Googlebot passed by on September 1, 2020 at 07:45:10

Googlebot coordinates the various crawling teams, which will typically come from data centers near the pages being indexed. In the robots.txt file, we tell Googlebot which pages to crawl. We can also use it to block crawlers from accessing part or all of our website. This robots.txt file must be located in the main directory of the server - for example, www.misitioweb.com/robots.txt.

Googlebot finds new pages by following links.

Indexing problems and difficulties

Googlebot will not be able to access content that requires a log-in or payment.
On the other hand, Flash, JAVA, Adobe Shockwave, audio and video files are content that Googlebot will generally not be able to crawl. In principle, Googlebot can only read text and is blind to everything else. Hence the use of ALT attributes, which we will see later.

The same is true for asynchronous JavaScript and XML, better known as AJAX. AJAX applications are problematic when it comes to crawling. It's best to avoid them whenever possible.

What should we do to get Google to index our content?

Getting Google to allow us to "register in the race" for its results, that is, to index our content, is relatively easy. All you have to do is communicate it directly through Google Search Console, https://search.google.com/search-console/

Tool that replaces Google Webmaster Tools.

Or you can link from an already indexed web page to the new web page we want to index in Google. When crawling the existing page, Googlebot will add the new page.

In order to get our content properly indexed, we'll need to keep this in mind and make it easier for Googlebot to process the most important texts. Also, Googlebot will not index a web page if it considers it a copy of an existing web page.

And once indexed, we must avoid at all costs that Google throws us out of its index. It will do so if it detects bad practices. Such de-indexing, much worse than a papal "excommunication", would throw us to civilian death on the Internet.

Being indexed allows us to run the marathon, although logically it does not guarantee that we will win it.

TIPS FOR SUCCEEDING WITH GOOGLE

Once we've developed a coherent strategy, and got Google to index our content, we move on to detailing what we need to do to get good results.

There are three types of factors to consider:

Those concerning the website. These are the structural factors.
Those that concern relevance. These are the internal factors.
Those that concern popularity. These are the external factors.

We'll start with the structural factors.

Advice on
Structural Factors

Tip 1

Register well

Google processes various data relating to the registration of a domain.

Name. Logically, Google has a "blacklist" of people who have a criminal, fraudulent or "spammer" history and penalizes the domains they register.

Concealment. Precisely because of the above, some of these individuals hide their data when registering, by means of different tricks, something that Google does not like.

Avoid registering a domain by hiding the data from the real registrar.

Expiration date

Google rewards domains that have a long expiration date. In fact, it says so in one of its patents:

"Legitimate domains often pay several years of their registration in advance, while illegitimate domains are rarely used for more than a year. "Therefore, the expiration date of a domain can be used as a factor to predict the legitimacy of a domain.

Therefore, whenever you can, register the domain for many years.

Tip 2

*Baptize with intelligence
(domain name)*

The first important decision we must make, if we launch a new website, is to choose the right domain name.

Empirical evidence from numerous searches indicates that the domain name does matter, even if Google does not like it, and has stated otherwise on countless occasions. From here we draw another lesson, we cannot trust everything Google says.

To this day, although its importance has shrunk over time, the domain name still carries some weight in Google's results.

The domain name alone, sometimes and usually for uncompetitive keywords, can make a web page rank high without optimizing other individual factors and without coming from a "prominent family" - that is, without being hosted on a very old website, a high number of inbound links and a high number of indexed pages. In other words, having the domain name can compensate for deficiencies in other areas.

What practical lesson can we draw from this result?

Well, if our goal is to achieve top positions for a large number of keywords, then clearly the domain name alone is not a relevant strategic factor. It is much more important as we will see to get a large number of inbound links or to create a powerful website, which receives many links and indexes a large number of pages.

Now, if our goal is to achieve top positions for a keyword -or several closely related ones- in an uncompetitive sector -let's forget about succeeding in tourism, hotels, travel, etc.- then it is important to choose a domain name that contains it, no matter how much Google repeats its mantra that it doesn't matter.

We can disprove Google with different searches that prove it.

For example, if we search for, The Way to Happiness, I don't know if we will find happiness, but there are several websites that contain those keywords in their domain.

The domain of the first search result

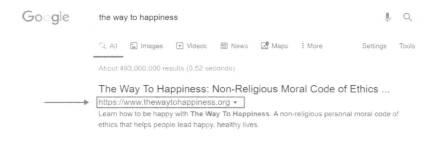

The domain of the first search result
The way to happiness

It is true that the importance of this factor has been greatly reduced, and continues to be reduced.

And in practice we have to be skilful in taking advantage of this criterion, since there are few domains available that contain interesting keywords, although there are new domain extensions -the final part of them- that still allow us to "fish" for something interesting.

Another area of the SEO universe where the domain name is

still important is in Google Mybusiness, that is, the results and searches of Google Maps, which are also sometimes inserted into the Google homepage. When sorting the Google Mybusiness tabs, the algorithm gives more weight to the domain name than for the general search, as it is also easily verifiable.

Let's now explain the rest of the structural factors, which usually receive much less attention than they deserve.

These are criteria associated with the website - as opposed to an individual web page. Google claims that, when ranking the results of its search response list, the basic element of its analysis is each web page. In this way, each and every web page competes with each other.

We will show that, although Google does not explicitly acknowledge this, it is once again failing to do so. The search engine attaches great importance to the website where the web pages are hosted, that is, to the "family" of each web page. To a large extent, Google has become more and more elitist. If a page is on an old, well-known website, the chances of it appearing in the top positions increase considerably. Just look, for example, at the number of Wikipedia pages that make it to the top of various searches - from common names to technical words to localities to celebrities. As we will see, there is a close relationship between the general website of a web page and its positions in Google. The following are positioning factors that depend on the general website.

Tip 3
Grow old or find yourself an old man (website age)

Another factor that depends on the website where a page is hosted is the age of that website. A mountain of evidence shows, overwhelmingly, that Google rewards pages hosted on relatively old websites and, in contrast, punishes pages hosted on recent websites. This behavior by Google is due to several simultaneous phenomena.

The first is the fight against junk websites, spam - a word that is a contraction of spiced ham, and which is applied either to fake emails or websites or junk, by a Monty Python film. Why does it do this? Because these websites are almost always recent. Spam professionals are constantly launching new websites. They trick users and search engines for a very limited period of time and then abandon that website as junk and launch a different website. Google has detected this procedure and has developed ways to counteract it by specifically penalizing pages hosted on new sites.

In addition to this hygienic measure, there are positive factors related to the age of the website, which indirectly favour the "old" ones. The most important of these are external inbound links, so logically, the older a website is, the more links it will have accumulated to it. Therefore, age is a very important factor. But what is its real importance? Can a new page get to the first position for some competitive keyword?

We have measured it through numerous studies, and the answer is that it is increasingly difficult, especially in competitive sectors.

If we look at my doctoral thesis, of the 359 web pages that

achieved the first position for 359 keywords on Google.com in 2012, only five of those web pages were hosted by a website less than three years old. **Therefore, 98.6% of the winning web pages (number 1) belonged to websites three years old or more. We have a fundamental fact, the average age of the websites where the web pages that would appear in the top positions were hosted was 8.15 years old.**

Has this changed over time? Yes, it has changed for the worse. You can be sure of that.

In 2018, I tutored Jorge Nuques in his final master's work, then a student in the (official) university master's degree in Digital Marketing, Communication and Social Networks, at the Universidad Camilo José Cela and the ID Digital School, which I run.

The main objective of this brilliant Master's work was to analyze the SEO criteria of the hotel sector, trying to identify the most relevant organic positioning factors within this sector.

Well, with regard to the age of the website, 99% of the websites in first position for hotel-related searches are over 3 years old, and their average age is 16.47.

Other research from 2016, 2017, 2018 and 2019 give very similar results.

We therefore see the extraordinary importance Google attaches to the age of the website where a web page is hosted. It is virtually impossible for a web page hosted on a new website to reach the top position in competitive search results.

There are other studies in the USA. The digital marketing tool Ahrefs, conducted a study in 2017, about how long it takes a website to achieve these competitive search results.

Conclusions of the study conducted with two million searches:

> • The web page that appears in the first position in the results in Google has an average of almost three years.
> • The websites in the top 10 positions have, on average, been in the top 10 for more than two years.
> • Only a meager 5.7% of all web pages in the top ten were less than one year old.

And all this, taking as a reference the age of the web page. But the most interesting thing, is to analyze the age of the website, as I have shown before. This is also done by the expert Ccarter, in the blog of Serpwoo, the digital marketing tool that analyzes competitive search results, in a study published in 2017.

https://www.serpwoo.com/blog/analysis/domain-age/

Results of your study? Here they are:

Search Term	Monthly Volume	Difficulty	Type	Youngest	Oldest	Average
Amazon	55,600,000	Short Tail	Brand	12.7	30.7	20,9
Apple	3,350,000	Short Tail	Brand	10.1	30.7	22,1
Beats By Dre	673	Short Tail	Brand	11.1	31.5	16,8
Beyonce	2,240,000	Short Tail	Celebrity	12.3	30.7	19,1
Black Friday Online Sales	2400	Long Tail	Discount	10.1	26.5	18,8
Boobs	1,220,000	Short Tail	Adult	4.9	22.5	17,5
Buy Garcina Cambogia	2,4	Short Tail	Buyer Intent	3.3	23.0	13,9
Buy Morphine Pills Online	50	Long Tail	Spammy	7.7 months	21.6	5,4
Buy Valium Online Legally	170	Long Tail	Spammy	1.8	20.5	7,9
Cheap Beats By Dre	14,8	Long Tail	Discount	1.6	30.7	16,9

Chicago SEO	1,9	Short Tail	Locality (Chicago, IL USA)	2.4	20.1	11,1
Chicago SEO Company	390	Short Tail	Locality (Chicago, IL USA)	3.8	20.1	11,4
Cyber Monday Sales	14800	Short Tail	Discount	4.9	24.1	17,4
Hotel	165	Short Tail	Generic	13.6	24.8	20,9
Kanye West	1,000,000	Short Tail	Celebrity	12.3	23.8	19,3
Keywords For Search Engine Optimization	20	Long Tail	Business Services	3.4	21.6	13,9
Keywords Suggestion Tool	20	Short Tail	Business Services	2.5	20.1	11,4
Kim Kardashian	3,350,000	Short Tail	Celebrity	5.5	30.7	19
Louis Vuitton Replica	5400	Short Tail	Spammy	10.7 months	23.0	14,3
Natalie Dormer	246	Short Tail	Celebrity	10.0	23.5	18,5
Online Pharmacy Ambien [2]	50	Short Tail	Spammy	6.8 months	20.1	4
Pay Per Click Management	140	Long Tail	Locality (Chicago, IL USA)	2.6	23.1	14,1
Search Based Keyword Tool	10	Long Tail	Business Services	3.4	20.1	13,7
Search Engine Marketing Professional	70	Long Tail	Business Services	5.4	23.2	15,5
Search Volume For Keywords	30	Long Tail	Business Services	1.0	20.1	11,9
SEO	90,5	Short Tail	Locality (Chicago, IL USA)	6.1	23.1	15,5
Social Media Competitive Analysis Tools	20	Long Tail	Business Services	3.0	22.4	10,2

The first column is the keyword, the second the volume of searches, the third if they are short tail (very difficult) or short tail terms. The next is the sector of the search - if they are brands, famous people, etc. - and the next is the age of the youngest result, i.e. the youngest, the oldest, and the average age of the first 20.

Good old Ccarter is so surprised that he does not dare to make the general average.

I did it. 14.68!

That is, the average age of the websites that host the web pages that manage to be in the top positions of Google, for competitive keywords is almost fifteen years old. That in Internet terms is an eternity. The first page of results is a geriatric.

Remember that in the study mentioned above, conducted in Google, the page that achieved the first position in hotel searches was hosted on a website that had, on average, 16.47 years. These are similar data, except that in the US we are talking about the first 20, not the first, which will certainly be older. The difference is explained by the higher level of competition in the US market compared to the Spanish one.

This reality may shock, scare or depress some SEO experts, but denying it will get us nowhere.

And once we know that Google rewards old web pages hosted on old websites, what can we do about it?

Well, it may be that our website is already old. If so, congratulations, you're much closer to getting positive results on Google - as long as the website hasn't been penalized in the past.

If that's not the case, we have two options. On the one hand, buy cheese and wine and sit back and wait for our website to age.

We may not have that much patience. Another option is, if we haven't yet chosen the domain where we will develop the website, to buy an old one. Before buying an old domain it is important to consider several factors:

On one hand, we must know that the most important thing regarding age, is not how many years a particular domain has been registered, but how many years it has been online, that is, uploaded to the Internet, with content indexed in Google. The latter is what really counts. Logically, what determines the age of a domain therefore is when it was first indexed, not when it was registered, because a domain may be undeveloped, in which case the passage of years does not count in its favor.

In addition, we must avoid domains that have a personality or identity of their own on the Internet that does not correspond to our project. Because Google will always associate them with that identity, affecting other search results. For example, we are not interested in a website that receives a large number of links with a certain anchor text, which is not related to our objectives.

And of course, we must avoid at all costs domains that are "tainted" in Google's eyes. These are domains that have suffered the wrath of the search engine. The most serious cases are those websites that are unindexed. Google has removed them from its results for doing something wrong, in the opinion of the search engine. We must avoid at all costs buying any of these "stinking" websites - they have suffered "civil death" on the Internet, much worse than the Papal excommunication.

There are also other websites which, without being unindexed, are penalised, to varying degrees, for carrying out bad practices which Google condemns.

Therefore, if we decide to buy an old website we must take precautions or risk that the remedy will be worse than the disease.

On the other hand, this factor also gives us clues about what we should NOT do. For example, throw away an old domain name and replace it with a new one. We can correctly redirect an old domain to a new one, but the change will have negative effects. If we do it wrong, disaster is guaranteed. This is a great lesson. Don't trade an old domain for a new one, keep the old one!

This mistake is made again and again by thousands of companies, institutions and enterprises.

In the face of this evidence, Matt Cutts, one of Google's spokesmen, has stated several times that the age of a domain only matters during the first few months.

Here too, Google is not telling the truth. The reality is that it has turned domains into good wine, which become better with age Or in virtual buildings that grow year by year. Replacing them with others is, at least partially, going back to the basics.

Tip 4

*Get links, links and more links
(number of inbound links to the
entire website)*

We're not done with structural factors. Another structural criterion, which concerns the website where a web page is hosted, is given by the number of external inbound links that the website receives.

That is, if we then see that the number of links -and their quality, along with other factors- that a specific webpage receives is important, so is the number and quality of links that the general domain, the website where that page is hosted, receives.

The research for my doctoral thesis is clear on this point. Of the 359 web pages analyzed in the first position for some keyword in Google, 69.36% of them are hosted by websites that receive, as a whole, more than 100,000 external links. For the 359, the average number of external links to their entire website is 93,088,761 links. Wikipedia, which receives a very high number of links, undoubtedly contributes to the high average.

In any case, these results confirm how important it is for the positioning of a web page to belong to a website that receives many external links. As if they were branches of a tree, there is therefore a clear relationship between the web page and the website where it is hosted.

A website like Wikipedia transmits its pagerank, prestige and popularity to its branches -the web pages- which explains why so many of its web pages manage to get good results.

In this way, as we have seen above, an individual web page can obtain PageRank and good positions in search results even without having external links, because if it is hosted on the right website, it receives an internal PageRank transfer.

Experts and specialized literature have not talked enough about this topic, which is of considerable importance. The main focus of the analysis has been on the individual web page, but as we have verified, it is necessary to analyse the whole website as well. Google, although it does not clearly recognise this, does.

What can we do about it?

It is clear that when we launch a website, we must ensure that that website as a whole receives a large number of external inbound links, to different web pages. To do this:

A) We must develop a lot of original content, as we will see later, spread over many web pages, which can attract links

B) We must structure the website properly, so that the Pagerank flows. There are many websites that do not transmit the PageRank well, for different reasons, so that the main portal -home- gets a high PageRank but is unable to pass it to other sections or pages of the same website.

It is necessary to develop the website correctly, so that the Pagerank flows throughout the length and width of the website, so that the main page - where the Pagerank is usually concentrated - reinforces the other web pages, and that these reinforce each other. This can be done by managing well how many sections are linked from the home page, and in turn how many pages receive links from the sections, etc.

We should not move the web pages too far from the home page, because then they receive little Pagerank and dry up.

Ideally, no page should be more than three levels away from the homepage. On the other hand, there should be no "slush funds" or dead-end pages on the website, because they mean a loss of return Pagerank.

This optimization of Pagerank is legitimate, although taken to excess it is punishable. These are link-sculpting or Pagerank Sculpting techniques. Part of these tricks were stopped when Google changed the Pagerank flow, altering the characteristics of the follow and non follow links.

Before, in the golden age of the wild west of SEO, if a homepage had four internal links, and three of them were nofollow, the fourth internal link would take all of Pagerank. In other words, a cannonball! Now that has changed, and the pagerank is divided between all the links, whether they are follow or not follow. This trick is over, but there are still others that are punishable and should be avoided.

C) In addition, our linkbuilding strategy should not focus on links to a single web page, but should succeed in generating links to different pages on our website.

Tip 5

Create lots of original content on your website (the more pages you have in-dexed on Google, the better)

Another factor that depends on the whole website, besides age and external links that reach the whole website, is the number of web pages of that website indexed in Google.

This figure will give us an idea of the importance of the website and the strength and authority it can convey to a web page.

To obtain this data, we can write the following in Google:

Site:X (domain name)

For example, if we write site:nytimes.com we get the number of web pages of The New York Times newspaper indexed in Google, which right now is over 8 million.

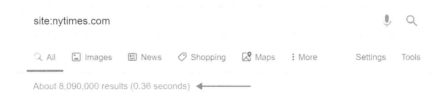

Number of web pages of the site "nytimes.com" indexed in Google

In my research, 66.3% of the winning websites - in the first position - were hosted by websites that have more than 100,000 pages indexed in Google. In subsequent research, this figure increases.

The average number of indexed pages on the websites of those winning pages is 52,445,151. Wikipedia certainly contributes to the high figure.

But even without counting wikipedia, we see that the average is 4,196,708.

In 2019 I was a tutor to Juan Prieto Rico, a student of the official master's degree in digital marketing, communication and social networks mentioned above, who wrote his brilliant final master's work (TFM) on key factors of organic positioning in the toy sector.

The websites that hosted the winning pages of different searches related to the toy sector had an average of 4,875,850 pages indexed in Google. And this is not counting Amazon, which raises the average, just like Wikipedia.

Perhaps this proven correlation is not causal, that is, a high number of contents indexed in Google does not in itself generate better positions, but for example generates a large number of inbound links that in turn improve positions.

In any case, like other structural factors before it, it deserves more attention than it has received to date.

And in view of this evidence, what can we do? Well, create a large number of web pages on our website, getting them indexed by Google. To do this we must provide them with original content and avoid duplicates. As a general rule, the more pages our website is indexed, the better. But always trying to have enough content, and from the respect to a general strategy that optimizes each web page for a different keyword.

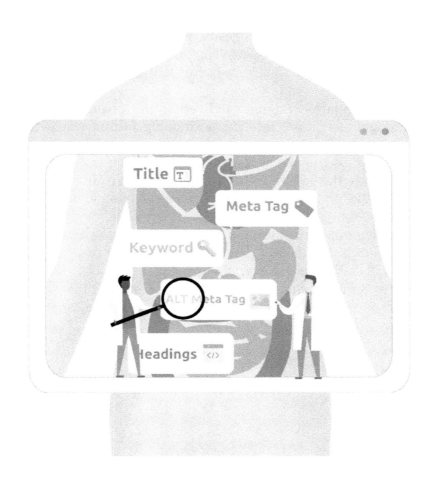

Advice on
Internal Factors

Here are some tips that will make our websites relevant to Google.

They refer to the internal positioning factors, called onpage - in the page - because they depend on the programming and contents of our own website. They are factors that we can manage.

If we compare obtaining good results in Google with building a skyscraper, these internal positioning factors would be the foundation. They are a necessary condition, not sufficient, to reach the top. If we make a mistake when building the foundations, which are the base of the skyscraper, it is very difficult for us to reach the top. But the foundation alone will not do it.

In order to optimize the internal factors, we must have strategically chosen which is the keyword or keywords of each web page. Then we will make sure that everything on that web page, from the title tag to the url, including the content, is focused on that keyword.

Tip 6
Tittle correctly

If we talk about internal SEO, the first thing we must do if we want to get somewhere in Google is to optimize the title tag.

The title tag is the text inside the <title>...</title> tags in the code of a web page. We can easily see the title tag of each page without accessing the code, since it's the text that appears at the top left in any browser when entering a web page. Also known as meta elements

For example, if we search meta-tags in Google, we first find the following website:

https://www.wikipedia.org/

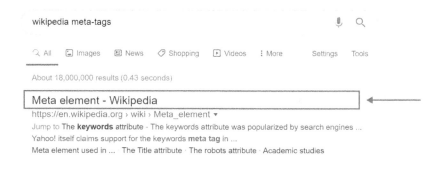

Here, the <title> tag is pointed out in a
Google search result

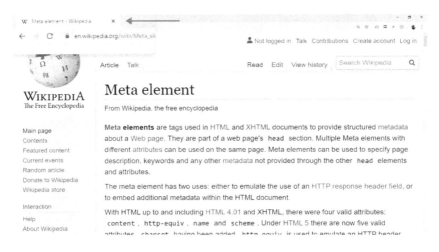

Here is the tag <title> on a web page

There is a general consensus among the various experts about how essential the presence of the keyword in the title tag of a web page is for it to appear in the first positions of the search for that keyword.

In different studies, the percentage of winning web pages (first position) that contain the searched keyword in its title tag is above 90%. 93% in Juan Prieto's research, 93.3% (335 out of 359) in my research, and 99% in Jorge Nuques' TFM.

There are few exceptions such as some websites that appear first for some animals such as dogs. Some of these exceptional cases are Wikipedia pages, which explains the anomaly since it is a very powerful website and has a particularly favourable treatment in Google results.

We can conclude that Google considers this positioning factor fundamental, and that *for a web page to achieve the first position for a given search it is a quasi-necessary condition that it contains that keyword in its title tag.*

Therefore, if we aspire to position a web page for a specific keyword, it is essential that it contains that keyword in its title tag.

Which brings us to another piece of advice. If we want to position our website for different keywords, ideally we should optimize different web pages for different keywords. As part of that optimization, each of the web pages should have a unique title tag, adapted to the specific keyword for which we want to position that web page.

For example, on the Atrapalo.com website we find the following page
https://www.atrapalo.com/vuelos/a-barcelona_bcn.html

Whose title tag is:
Vuelos a Barcelona BCN

This is an example of how to properly manage the title tag.

Other related tips:

• **Place the priority keywords at the beginning of the title tag.** If you also want to use the name of a company, brand or the general website, do it behind the keyword.

• **Limit the total length of the title tag to 65 characters (with space), which is what Google processes.**

• **Use several keywords** if necessary, in case that web page is optimized for several terms or you think it brings something to it. For example, a title can be "treadmills, treadmills" if the web page aims to position itself for both keywords.

• **Incorporate the searcher's intention** into the tag,

whenever possible. For example, if someone wants to buy a gas boiler, the title might be "gas boilers: buy and install your boiler".

• **Be consistent** throughout the website. Make sure that all title tags follow the same pattern on all your web pages.

Follow the tag

There are other recommendations regarding tags that are worth following if you want a web page to be optimized in the eyes of Google.

The meta description tag is a text that appears only in the code of the web page. When entering the web page, the user does not see it. That text is supposed to succinctly reflect what the web page in question is about. But in addition to being read into the code by crawlers, it's unique in that it's the text that usually appears in Google's search results. The user will see it only at that moment, not when entering the webpage.

Here is the meta description tag in a Google search result

In general, relative importance is given to the meta description label.

In our empirical study, 36.5% of the web pages contain the keyword in their meta description tag. As a qualitative data, it is worth mentioning that the ones that use it the most are web pages in first positions of very competitive keywords -travels, flights, contacts, casino, offers, sex, hotels, video games. So we can conclude that the meta description tags have some importance.

The web page that aspires to reach outstanding positions in Google should therefore optimize the meta description tag for the target keyword - for which it wants to be positioned.

Besides helping to position the website, it has an additional benefit, since in the search results the keyword contained in the meta description tag will appear in bold - which increases the chances of the user clicking.

On the other hand, it is convenient that the meta description tag does not exceed 160 characters processed by Google.

Meta Keywords Tag

The Meta Keyword tag allows you to define which terms are important for the website. It should be placed between the <head>...</head> tags of the HTML code of the Web page.

Example: <meta name="keywords" content="keyword, other keyword">

In my research, 26% of the web pages contain the keyword in the meta keyword tag. More than a quarter of the top pages use these tags, which many experts describe as obsolete.

In 2012 Matt Cutts said that Google would consider meta keyword tags for its Google News algorithm when ranking news, but no longer for the general webpage algorithm. Do we trust what Google says?

In Juan Prieto's 2019 study of the toy industry, almost 60% of the winning websites use that meta tag, although that percentage drops to 27% if we remove the results from Amazon, which does use them.

In any case, it doesn't bother and it costs little to put it up, considering that assuming it still counts for something, it is a factor that counts little by itself.

ALT Tag

The <img alt> attribute defines an alternative text for an image when the user uses a text browser or disables image viewing in his web browser. Internet Explorer displays that alternative text if the user puts the cursor over the image.

This is another criterion that should be taken into account, although it is of little importance to Google.

In my research, 34.8% of web pages contained the keyword in the alt tag. In the TFM research for the toy sector the percentage rises to 80%, while in Jorge Nuques' TFM for the hotel sector, the percentage is 59%.

If an image cannot be displayed for some reason, the ALT attribute provides alternative text to display instead.

Like the previous one, it costs very little to put it on and it brings something.

Tip 8

Create quality, original and specialized content

Google has been repeating for years that content is king in determining its search results. Supposedly, the best way to reach high positions is to create useful and interesting content for users.

Knowing that as we have already seen Google does not always - or rather almost never - tell the whole truth about its algorithm, it is interesting to discern whether content is indeed an important factor, and what characteristics it should have.

Content par excellence is the text of a web page.

What should be its ideal length? How many words should the text of the web page have? Can there be a page with very little text that gets into the first position in Google?

In my research, 81.6% of the websites in the top positions contain 200 or more words of text. However, it is interesting to note that there were 66 web pages - 18.4% of the total number of cases studied - that obtained a first position in the search result and yet contained less than 200 words of text.

It should be noted that 21 of these web pages were hosted on the website www.wordreference.com, which has a lot of strength and is favoured by Google, which treats its results well. Many of the remaining web pages contained the keyword within their domain name, which gave them additional strength.

On the other hand, 72.1% of the analyzed web pages contained more than 300 words. And 49.9% of the web pages in the top positions were above 700 words of text.

The length of the text ranged from the zero words detected at that time in the text of http://www.pajareriateodoro.com/index2.htm -due to its programming, which allowed the human eye to see text but not the spiders of the search engines- to the 26,942 words contained in the Wikipedia entry about art, http://es.wikipedia.org/wiki/Arte, which managed to appear in first place when we were searching for the keyword art, seven years ago, just as it does now.

We should note that the 15 web pages that contained the most text in that study were Wikipedia entries. The average number of words per page, for all the cases analyzed, was 2,108.

However, in view of some web pages that snuck into the first positions with hardly any text -almost 18.4% of the total cases studied at the time obtained a first position in the search result and yet contained less than 200 text words- if content is king, Google was at times Republican. It was common that most of those web pages contained the keyword in whole or in part in the domain name.

Google has become more monarchical, and those web pages now have more than 200 words, or have ceased to be in the first position. Those with less than 400 have the keyword in the domain for the most part.

In later studies, the importance of having an extensive text is confirmed. In Juan Prieto's research, the average is 2061. All of them have more than 400 words. The one that less had 457 words.

In Jorge Nuques' research, for the hotel sector, the average is 3192 words. In this study, all of the winning pages have a text length of more than 200 words, and 96% of the results have more than 300 words. There are four that have between 200 and 300 words, and they are web pages that contain the keyword totally or partially in the domain name.

This is an important finding, since some experts recommend limiting the number of words in the text of web pages, advice that is revealed, in view of this result, dispensable. Rather, the opposite should be recommended. In light of the results, it is desirable for a web page to have extensive text - as long as it is relevant, as is the case with Wikipedia pages, and to maintain reasonably high densities.

It is clear that the length of text is not therefore a parabolic factor - there is a point beyond which increasing the text is counterproductive - but rather linear - the more text the better, provided that an appropriate keyword density is maintained - this we will see later.

This is corroborated by a recent study by ahrefs:

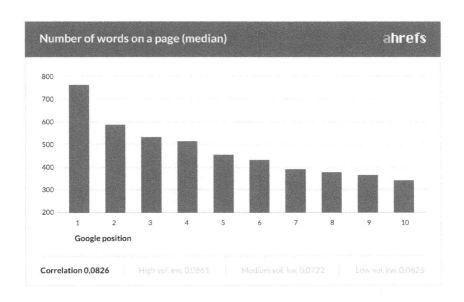

Number (average) of words on a page -vs- Position in Google

Other advice

It is also desirable that the content of the website includes some outgoing links to quality websites. This gives Google confidence about the quality of the content.

That is, just as it penalizes links to toxic (Badrank) websites, Google likes a website to link to reliable places.

Tip 9

Write dense

It seems logical to think that Google will give a bonus to those web pages that have textual relevance for a given keyword. If a user searches for Horses in Google, we will intuitively expect that the pages that appear in prominent positions will contain descriptive texts that repeat a number of times the word "horse" or "horses" or their synonyms -even though it is a textual and not really semantic search engine, Google is capable of processing synonyms as if they were the word being searched for.

This criterion is called keyword density in the text of the page, and is the result of dividing the number of times a particular keyword appears by the total number of words in the text of that web page.

Now, logically we can think that the designer of a web page, knowing the importance of this textual relevance, fills in the text of the page with the keyword in which he is most interested in standing out. That way, a web page about trips to Morocco could put those words -Travel, Morocco, trips to Morocco- all over the text, so that they are repeated many times. This practice is called keyword stuffing and is penalized by Google.

Therefore, here we are clearly dealing with a positioning factor with a parabolic effect. Google's algorithm rewards a reasonable density of a keyword in the text of the page, but penalizes abnormal or manipulated densities.

Experts who know the nature of this factor have traditionally stated that the ideal density of the keyword in the text of the page ranges from 2% (the word in question is repeated twice for every hundred words) to 7% (the word is repeated seven times for every hundred words).

It is therefore of great interest to study the following two issues:

a) What is the ideal percentage of keyword density in the text of a web page?

b) What is the maximum percentage of density that allows a web page to be placed in the first places?

The approximate answer to this first question will be given by the average of all the web pages in the first position in google for the different keywords.

We will see if that percentage is within the range that is often shuffled - between 2% and 7% - and that we could consider the scientific consensus on this.

The maximum densities on the pages in the first positions will give us the answer to the second question.

In other words, we will see which are, irrespective of the average, the highest densities that manage to get to the top.

In my research, the average density of all the web pages in the first positions studied is 2.35% (of every hundred words of text on the web page, the keyword is repeated a little more than twice).

The density of all of them ranged from 0% to 21.56%.

At that time there were only 11 winning pages with keyword density in the text above 7%. These were the following web pages:

Palabra clave	Página web	Densidad
lengua	http://es.wikipedia.org/wiki/Lengua	7,27
mercedes	http://www.mercedes-benz.es/	7,89
gamo	http://es.gamo.com/	8,42
aries	www.euroresidentes.com/horoscopos/signos/signo-aries.htm	9,79
valencia	http://www.valencia.es/	10
moviles	http://www.moviles.com/	10,9
dosal	http://www.dosal.cl/	11,19
botin	http://www.botin.es/	12,12
empleo	http://www.empleo.com/	12,61
apartamentos	http://www.niumba.com	15,54
coliflor	http://www.arecetas.com/coliflor/index.html	21,56

Of those, the only ones that remain in first position with high densities are the language entry of Wikipedia, the Mercedes-Benz website and gamo.com, which has a density above 7% for the word gamo. All three are explainable exceptions to the general rule, as they are two brands and one Wikipedia page.

This result confirms that a density above 7% makes it very difficult or almost impossible to get a good result in Google.

On the other hand, there were 199 web pages with densities below 2% and 78 web pages with densities below 1%, which achieved the first position.

We can say that a density of less than 1% makes it difficult to achieve a first position in Google, although we must add that, in certain circumstances, it does not prevent it. **75.2% of the pages in first place at that time had densities between 1% and 7%.**

This data is corroborated by ulterior studies. The average density of all of them is between 2% and 3%, counting synonyms.

There are more, not all sectors are the same, some will have more density than others. One piece of advice would be to analyze the densities of the results in the first positions, for example, the average of the first three. This will give you an idea of what the ideal density is in your sector. You can do this with several tools, one of them, free of charge, is the SEOQUAKE extension that is free and can be installed in different browsers. It can also be used to analyse other data, as we have seen.

Therefore, if you want your website to reach the top positions, use a text that has a keyword density of around 2%, not exceeding 7% or falling below 1%. Of course, you should also take into account the sector you are in, since this percentage can vary.

Another tip: use synonyms, you'll be telling Google that your content is quality.

Tip 10

Use the headings well

Headings or hierarchy tags (from H1 to H6) are the types of text highlighted on a web page. The HTML code allows six different types of hierarchy above the normal text. There is a general consensus that it is important that the desired keyword is highlighted in these headings on a web page. The use of these specific header marks gives Google clues about what the designer considers important.

Not all headings are equally important. Logically, the H1 is more important than the H2, and so on.

The JustWatch site uses only one H1

It is necessary to start by having only one H1 on each page, which should reflect the main keyword for which we want to optimize that page. If we have two different H1s on the same page, we are sending contradictory signals to the search engine, and to some extent also to the user.

Pages that are in the top positions usually contain the keyword in their H1.

You can also use the H2 to include secondary or tertiary keywords. And if it makes sense, use other headings, but don't saturate the web page with unnecessary or contradictory headings.

Tip 11

Optimize the URL

A url, or Uniform Resource Locator, is the address of a web page.

For example,
http://en.wikipedia.org/wiki/Uniform_Resource_Locator

This is the url of the Wikipedia entry that defines what a url is.

While http://www.google.com/chrome?hl=es is the url of the page to download the Spanish version of Chrome, Google's browser.

The urls are also text, and therefore are crawled by search engines. When the keyword is not in the main domain - which is the first part of the url, for example www.google.com in the example above, it is important that it is at least somewhere in the url.

In my research, 88.3% of the web pages in the top positions contain the keyword in their url. In later studies, this figure is even higher.

As was the case with the keyword in the title tag - let us remember that about 93% of the web pages in the top positions contain the keyword in their title tag - the presence of the keyword in the url of a page is therefore practically a sine qua non for achieving top positions in Google searches.

So, for example, let's look at what the website www.vuelosbaratos.es does. The website that talks about cheap flights to Belgium and Brussels is http://www.vuelosbaratos.es/vuelos-a-bruselas-bélgica.htm

It contains the keywords of interest in its url. The website has a web page for each potential combination of keywords - flights to mallorca, ibiza, tenerife, etc.

Advice on External Factors

Having studied the internal factors, related to relevance, we will now look at the factors that make a website popular. These are external factors.

Tip 12
Get link juice (PageRank)

In practically every event about Google, search engine positioning or SEO -search engine optimization-, there is talk of an enigmatic element: PageRank. The PageRank bar became famous among webmasters, who proudly wielded or lamented the magic number it gave to each website. I speak in the past tense because although Pagerank is still very important, Google does not show it now.

But what exactly is the PageRank of a website? How does it influence Google's search results? What can we do about it?

Google itself defines PageRank as: "PageRank is based on the unique democratic nature of the web and uses its extensive link structure as an indicator of the value of an individual page. Google interprets a link from page A to page B as a vote by page A for page B."

But Google checks many other aspects besides the number of votes or links a page receives, since it also analyzes the web page that casts the vote. The votes cast by pages that are themselves "important" weigh more heavily and help make other pages "important" as well. PageRank therefore counts the number of inbound links, but also weighs up the quality of those links. And all that at the same time, for the whole Internet.

The concept of PageRank emanates from the founders of Google themselves. The idea was revolutionary at the time and we can think that it is still the hard core of the DNA of the Google algorithm.

It is considered a good PageRank from 3/10. Very few websites have a PageRank above 6/10. Only Google and very few pages achieve 10. In Spain , the university portal universia.es reached a PageRank of 10, while the main media have between 6 and 9 (Elmundo.es)

It is much easier, as we will see, to go from a PageRank of 0 to a PageRank of 1, than to go from 1 to 2, and so on, since the distance between the different levels is not linear.

Google usually updates the PageRank value from time to time, for its internal use, because I have already explained that now it does not show it anymore.

The founders of Google explain the PageRank in detail in a document published in 1998.

There they say that "one can think of a link as an academic quote. Therefore, a major web page like http://www.yahoo.com/ will have tens of thousands of inbound links (or citations) pointing to it" (The PageRank Citation Ranking: Bringing Order to the Web, (Sergei Brin and Larry Page, 1998)

We will not explain here the very complex mathematical operations that allow calculating the PageRank of a page. They are explained by Amy Langville and Carl D. Meyer, in their work, "PageRank and beyond, the science of search engine rankings" (2006), but it will be enough to indicate that the PageRank depends on:

• The number of inbound links to the web page in question
• The quality of these inbound links (the PageRank of the pages that send the link)
• The number of other outgoing links to other pages on the pages that send the link. If the page you link to has many outgoing links, the "strength" of that link is less. In fact, the "strength" that a page sends is divided among all the outbound links it has. For a while, it was only divided among the follow

links, but since Google changed it - and with it, as we have seen, reduced the possibilities of manipulating the flow of Pagerank - it is divided among all the links, be they follow or nofollow.

To better understand what this is about, we can compare the link system with an irrigation system. The PageRank would be the total amount of water that reaches a given field -website- at a given time, through multiple pipes -links. If the water you receive through a pipe comes from a reservoir with numerous pipes to other fields, obviously less water arrives. The quality of the water will depend on the quality of the swamps. A website, composed of numerous web pages, also has an internal system of "irrigation" and redistribution of the PageRank - water. On the one hand, a considerable amount of PageRank is transferred from the home page to the internal web pages. On the other hand, each page created is a small tributary, and the more pages you have, the more water will reach the home page of the web site. That partly explains why websites in, for example, news, have a high PageRank, since they have a large number of pages and internal links that flow to the home site. They also have many inbound links, to the home page and many of their pages.

We can also think of PageRank as a system of references and academic credits. The more an author -a web page- receives, the better, but it will count who gives the reference -it's not the same thing as an eminent person who is much less reputable- and it will also count -or at least it should count- the ease with which an expert gives good references about the work of others -in other words, if he quotes thousands of authors or only a few.

How important is the PageRank?

Google said again and again that webmasters and website managers should not be obsessed with PageRank, because it is one of many factors.

The reality is that it is still one of the most important factors, quite possibly the most important. For my research I was still able to analyze the published Pagerank, and confirm that the PageRank of a web page strongly influences the positions of that page in the Google results. But how much exactly? In the sample, 85.8% of the 359 top-ranked web pages for different keywords had a PageRank of 3 or more. That is, 308 pages out of 359. The average PageRank (in slash) was 4.6.

We can therefore conclude that, no matter what Google says, to reach a first position in its results for a keyword it is essential to have a high PageRank - equal or higher than 3.

We have seen that the PageRank, in its original formulation, is achieved through incoming links to a specific web page. However, some websites manage to have a considerable Pagerank with hardly any external inbound links. They achieve this by being hosted on websites that receive numerous external inbound links. We therefore see that these pages receive internal PageRank flows, which come from their own websites.

We also know that there are other factors, besides the number of inbound links to the page and the internal link flow, that affect PageRank.

Tip 13
Get them to trust you - Trustrank

This is where the so-called Trustrank comes in, which is a system originally devised by Stanford University and Yahoo! (described in this study[8]), to combat spam on the Internet, and to be able to distinguish between good and bad links.

It involves choosing a number of reputable websites, and designing a way to automatically give more weight to the links coming from that select "club" of websites. We know that Google includes within its PageRank calculation - or in parallel with it - a TrustRank component that depends on the quality of the websites that link to a given web page. That would partly explain why Wikipedia pages have overwhelmingly - even those that do not enjoy numerous external links - a high PageRank and obtain excellent positions in search results. Google gives all of them "a boost" in its results, because it trusts Wikipedia, and on the other hand the website excels in several structural factors such as age, number of pages indexed and the total number of links it receives.

The advice - as we will see later - is key. It is necessary to get quality links from websites that Google "trusts".

[8] http://ilpubs.stanford.edu:8090/770/1/2004-52.pdf

Tip 14

*Run away from bad company -
BadRank*

At the opposite conceptual end of the PageRank - it affects you negatively - we come across the BadRank. If the PageRank of our particular website goes up when you receive links from other websites, which transfer part of their own PageRank to us, the BankRank works very differently. It is based on the links that we place on our website to websites that Google considers undesirable. The search engine penalizes the links that we place from our website - which we control - to those "undesirables". That is the BadRank, which undoubtedly lowers the PageRank of a particular web page. The BadRank is therefore the consequence of linking from our website to "bad neighborhoods" on the Internet - which in turn have a high BadRank. Google penalizes us for associating our website with the bad guys.
When we put a link on our website to a high BadRank website, some of this negative flow comes back to us.

It is likely that Google will calculate the BadRank and PageRank separately, and then somehow subtract that from it - or split them.

The proof that BadRank exists is given by a considerable number of web pages that receive a PageRank of 0, despite enjoying numerous external and internal inbound links. Somehow that positive PageRank is neutralized by negative BadRank.

If we had to reduce all this to a formula, we could say that:

$$PRf = PRi * TR - BR$$

Where: PRf = final PageRank, PRi = initial PageRank (number

and quality of links), TR = TrustRank and BR = BadRank

This means that when calculating PageRank, Google analyses in depth the quality of the links a web page receives and also the links that this page sends to other web pages. In addition, Google also penalizes links that we may receive from pirates, spammers or other Internet outcasts - even if it is not strictly our fault. This has had a perverse effect that must be taken into account. This is negative SEO, a bad practice that consists of deliberately linking from "bad" websites to a competitor's website. These are often websites hosted in China and Russia. Sometimes we have found clients who have suffered in their flesh from this malpractice, which can have a very negative influence. It can be remedied. We must analyze in detail what all these links are and ask Google to disregard them, again through Search Console.

PageRank from 0 to 10 versus actual PageRank

It should also be noted that the number from 0 to 10 of PageRank reflected in the meter of this famous Google bar is not arithmetic, but exponential or logarithmic. The Pagerank shown in the bar, as a value between 0 and 10 was a simplification that Google made of the real Pagerank, which is a much higher number, since it has an exponential factor -let's assume it's 8, although we don't know that for sure. In other words, from 1 to 2 of Pagerank in the Google bar, there are eight times more "strength". The actual PageRank values would look like this:

PageRank in bar	Real PageRank
0	0,15 a 1,2
1	1,2 a 9,6
2	9,6 a 76,8
3	76,8 a 614,4
4	614,4 a 4.915,2
5	4.915,2 a 39.321,6
6	39.321,6 a 314.572,8
7	314.572,8 a 2.516.582,4
8	2.516.582,4 a 20.132.659,2
9	20.132.659,2 a 161.061.273,6
10	161.061.273,6 to infinite

Author's table showing Google Toolbar PageRank and its actual equivalent, assuming a factor of 8.

With these data, we can associate to each number of bar PageRank a number of real PageRank, calculated as the average of the fork in each case. In this way we would have the following:

PageRank in bar	Real PageRank value (average)	Real PageRank
0	0,675	0,15 a 1,2
1	5,4	1,2 a 9,6
2	43,2	9,6 a 76,8
3	345,6	76,8 a 614,4
4	2764,8	614,4 a 4.915,2
5	22118,4	4.915,2 a 39.321,6
6	176947,2	39.321,6 a 314.572,8
7	1415577,6	314.572,8 a 2.516.582,4
8	11324620,8	2.516.582,4 a 20.132.659,2
9	90596966,4	20.132.659,2 a 161.061.273,6
10	*	161.061.273,6 to infinite

Author's table showing the average actual PageRank value for each PageRank value in the Google Toolbar.

Let's see what happens if we replace the bar PageRank value with that average real PageRank value, in each of the 359 results of our research.

The average real PageRank, calculated in this way, is 645,802.3. As we see in the table above, this value falls within the real PageRank box of 7. It is logical that this is so, since having a base of 8, the higher PageRanks raise the average - which is 4.6 for bar PageRank and 7 for real PageRank.

Correlations of the real PageRank variable

We know that the actual PageRank variable is positively related to the number of inbound links to the web page and website. Also, with the age of the website where the page is hosted. The older it is, the more PageRank. You pray because you receive more inbound links over time, or because in the calculation of PageRank, Google considers not only the inbound links but also the age of the website, as a confidence factor, as well as the age of the links.

Tip 15
Get yourself linked up

As mentioned above, the number of external inbound links a website receives is the basis of its PageRank and the most important of the so-called external - in English, off-page - positioning factors.

By inbound links we mean links or hypertexts from other websites that lead to the website we are analysing.

The SEOmoz institute, which specialises in search engine optimisation (SEO) techniques, carries out a study based on interviews with experts from all over the world about the most important elements of search engine algorithms. It conducts interviews with a large number of experts and also carries out a statistical analysis of results.

In their latest study (source: http://www.seomoz.org/article/search-ranking-factors#ranking-factors) from 2015, both the experts and the study concluded that the most important factors for positioning on Google were the quantity and quality of external links to the website.

If we go to our research, the average was more than eighty-three thousand -83,243- inbound links to each web page that occupies the first position, so we can conclude as a priori that a high number of inbound links are needed to achieve the first position in Google's results for a given keyword.

So what can we do about it?

We already know how important PageRank is for a website to achieve top positions in Google. And we know that it is related to the number of links it receives. So, what can we do about it?

Links, links, links

On the one hand, we are sure that the more links our website receives, the better. The higher the PageRank will be, and the possibilities that page has to reach outstanding positions in the search results. However, there are a number of criteria to be taken into account.

To begin with, it is essential that the web page that sends us the link is indexed in Google. If it is not, that link does not count.

Secondly, we know that the webpage that links to us should not be hosted on a "toxic" website or else Google will penalize us.

Under these conditions, it is important to get, in one way or another, as many links as we can.

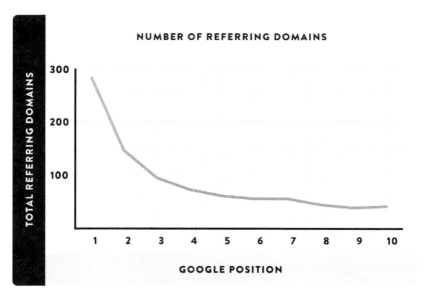

Domains that send links -vs- Position in Google

Generation of links (Linkbuilding)

This is where the famous term linkbuilding comes in.
How do we get links? The first thing we have to do is to ask all our friends and acquaintances for them. It seems obvious, but some people don't do it.

Ask everyone you know who has access to a website to link to you!

After that, we have to launch a coherent strategy of "linkbuilding" or what is the same, of obtaining links.

1) Directory links. Obtaining links from directories, whether paid or free, is an old - in relative terms, of course - link acquisition strategy. Its effectiveness is currently quite limited. I won't say nil, but almost, since Google has long since taken away the power of directory links. The only exceptions are links from highly reputable directories, which serve as references for Google, because they are human-edited directories - inclusion in these directories is not automatic, but there is a selection and verification process. Some reputable directories are paid for. For example, Yahoo had a very prestigious directory, which is now inactive. Yelp is an example of an important local directory that is still in operation.

2) Write. A good way to get links is to write articles or other publications on interesting topics, and add a link to them somewhere in the text. There are a number of websites that reproduce articles, or blog entries, and therefore generate links. Here, too, Google has been getting its act together, and it takes away the power of links that are generated in this way, even though they still count for something.

3) Produce videos, applications, extensions or other

content. With the same logic as articles or other texts, if we produce interesting content we can generate links to our website, provided that these contents contain the appropriate hyperlink to our website. This is what they call linkbait, that is to say, "link hooks", which are launched with the intention that their distribution among a large number of users generates links to our website.

4) Link exchange management. Rare is the administrative contact of a website that has not received an email requesting a reciprocal link exchange. This is a barter proposal, often automated. You link to me, I link to you and so everyone is happy. Google, however, has long known that this is a barter, and it detracts from the value of reciprocal links with similar characteristics, which "smell" like a link exchange.

5) News. One way to generate links is through the generation of news. We write a press release and try to get it published by the media related to the news or news agencies. We can also publish it on paid news broadcast platforms.

6) Comments. We can write comments that include inbound links in forums, blogs, news, etc. The value of these comments is small, but they are still indexed by Google and therefore count.

7) Buy. Google prohibits the purchase of links. As long as there are people who sell them, there will be people who can buy them. It is true that they themselves have violated this policy in the past, for example in 2012, when the advertising team of Chrome - owned by Google - bought links to the browser download page until it was discovered and penalized by Google itself after the scandal was mounted. It is also true that it is very difficult for Google to detect this practice, which is very common. However, my duty is to warn of the risks involved, because if Google detects it, it can punish the offender.

Quantity and quality

We've already seen that the more links we generate, the better. However, we must be aware that quality also counts. On the one hand, the higher quality links will give us more PageRank. On the other hand, there are links that convey authority, credibility, trust, because they have a high TrustRank. When we receive a link from a website with a high reputation, this transfers part of that positive reputation to us as well.

The anchor-text is fundamental

In addition to the number and quality of links, it is essential to pay attention to the text associated with those links, i.e. the anchor text, which is the visible text on a web page. This is the text that is generally in blue and can be clicked on.

Google will associate a web page with the anchor text of the links that this web page receives. For example, if we search in Google right now: Click here

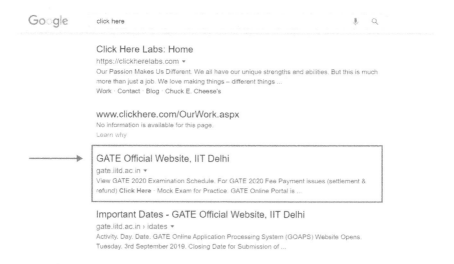

It appears in a prominent position in the results, the website: http://gate.iitd.ac.in/

A priori, that website has little relevance for the search, and is not optimized in any of the criteria we have seen, for that keyword.

Why is it in the top positions?

Because many websites that link to that website, and on those links, it says "click here"

Google processes those links, and associates the page with the text of those links.

This is what explains the concept of "Google bombs".

What is a Google bomb?

It is a concerted action by a number of computer scientists that allows certain web pages to be placed at the top of the results of a Google search using a given keyword. This is achieved by including links to the web page that is the object of the "Google bomb" in as many different pages as possible, so that the text of the link is the desired search criterion -keyword-.

Like so many other things inherent in Google, the company claims to have solved the problem in January 2007. But it has not. There are Google bombs and there will be, although it is now more complicated to achieve them.

There is evidence of many Google bombs after January 2007. Among the recent ones, it is worth noting that in July 2018 images of the current US President, Donald Trump, appeared for the "idiot" search. In November 2018 and August 2019, images of Pakistan's Prime Minister Imran Khan appeared in the bhikhari (a word meaning "wanderer" in the Hindi and Urdu languages) search. In February 2019, the search for "best toilet paper in the world" featured the flag of Pakistan.

So, we see that however much Google refines its algorithm, there are inherent elements that cannot be changed. The bombs are still there and will be there for the forseeable future-forever.

What is certain is that Google can now detect illogical or unnatural patterns of anchor text, if for example it suddenly processes a large number of links that have exactly the same anchor text.

It is therefore advisable, when trying to link to our website, that these have varied anchor texts. These can be synonyms - Google processes them appropriately - or variations of the same text, through different phrases, but it is not advisable to generate a large number of links with exactly the same anchor text.

For example, if you want to promote the homepage of a travel agency specialising in Morocco, instead of getting a large number of links with the anchor text "travel to Morocco", it is preferable to get links containing different anchor texts: "travel to Morocco", "travel in Morocco", "travel around Morocco", "find the best trip to Morocco", "the best trips to Morocco", "travel", "Morocco", etc. Google will look favourably on this anchor-text pattern, and will be suspicious if it suddenly processes a large number of links to that web page with exactly the same anchor-text "travel to Morocco".

Location of the link within the page

On the other hand, the location of a link within a web page is becoming increasingly important. Links located in prominent parts of a web page do not count the same as links located at the bottom of the page. The most noble part of a page, in Google's eyes, is the upper left-hand side. Similarly, a contextual link within a text will be more natural and valid a priori than one that appears in isolation, outside the main text of a web page.

Phases, deadlines and scales

Similarly, Google analyses the time factor in the increase of links to a website, so it will suspect - and penalise - those websites that suddenly receive a large number of links. In this way it tries to prevent the massive purchase and sale of links. Besides the fact that buying links is forbidden by Google, buying a large number of links at once is a particularly bad idea, because Google is likely to detect it.

Also, if Google sees a sudden decrease in the number of links to a website, it will suspect that someone is playing dirty, and will act accordingly.

Age of the links

Another important factor is the age of the links. Spammers", which are those websites that want to trick Google, create a lot of web pages and sudden links. As a result, Google is suspicious of web pages hosted on new websites - we have already seen that - but it is also suspicious of new links. On the contrary, it favours links that are more than one month old, especially those that are more than six months old.

Several conclusions and tips can be drawn from this approach by Google.

1) Links that have been pointing to a website for a long time should not be changed, unless we have a very good reason to do so.
2) Google always works with a bit of a "delay" with regard to link management. If we generate them today, we will see the effects in one, two, three or more months. Likewise, if we remove some links, the favourable inertia will last for a while, and the effects will not be immediate.
3) Another tip is to avoid the practice known as linkchurning - which would translate as link jumbling or shaking - which

consists of automatically making and unmaking links. That way the links do not get old, and therefore Google does not like them.

Pagerank distribution of the links

It is also necessary that the links that a web page receives come from pages following a logical PageRank distribution pattern. What does this mean? It means that on the Internet there is a natural distribution of PageRank among the different web pages. For example, there are many more web pages that have a PageRank of 0 or 1 than web pages that have a PageRank of 2 or 3. And so on, there are very few of 7, 8, 9 or 10. Google will "smell this cake". And it will do everything but grace.

It is therefore necessary to generate links that follow a logical pattern, from a PageRank point of view, and to avoid generating an excessive number of high PageRank links without a counterbalance of low PageRank links.

How to evaluate a potential link

If we want to evaluate the convenience of getting a link from a specific website to one of ours, it is convenient to review the following:

1) The PageRank of the web page where the link to our website will be.
2) The number of outgoing links from the web page that would link to us. The more you have, the less PageRank will go to ours.
3) The authority and reliability of the main website of the website from which you will link to our website
4) The relevance of the website in general and the specific content of the website that would link us, with respect to the theme of our website. If they talk about the same thing, it's

more interesting.

5) The part of the page where the link to our website would appear.

6) The quality of the links near that place

7) The context text that will be linked to the link.

We can also be helped by tool indicators, for example those we have seen before from SEMrush, which will tell us the confidence and authority of the page and the domain.

Other Tips

Tip 16
If you're social, better

In addition to all the factors explained so far, which are the main ones, there are other factors that Google also takes into account. At the moment they are relatively unimportant, but they are increasing.

Google is constantly trying to increase the usefulness of its search results. When it perceived, at the beginning of 2010, the inexorable importance of social networks, it began to take them into account as "signs" of classification in its results. In December 2010, Google officially commented that it already took into account the main social networks. On February 24, 2011, the so-called Panda update confirmed that this is the case. This trend has continued.

Social networks therefore have a double impact on Google's results:

A) On the one hand as links, they have the same validity as a link in similar circumstances. Social networks generate a large number of links to a web page, although as they come from the same website - for example from Twitter, Google gives them limited importance.

B) Signals. The different social indicators help Google to know if a website has social importance. Also to know if it has "freshness", a characteristic especially relevant for some searches, to which Google includes a component called QDF - "query deserves freshness" in English, which can be translated in Spanish as "la búsqueda merece frescura". These are searches that are newsworthy or have many changes - a famous character, a sports result, etc. In principle, the strength of a "signal" is much less than a link, because a signal is much easier to emit - it costs much more effort to place a link on a web page than to click on a social network. That's why Google has said that interaction on social networks - sharing, liking, etc. - is not a direct factor in ranking. This means precisely that, that a "like" on a social network is not equivalent to a link. In contrast, Bing says it does consider it a direct factor.

If we analyze a recent study by Cognitive SEO, we see that there is a positive relationship between presence, activity and interaction in social networks (share, comment, like) and the position in Google.

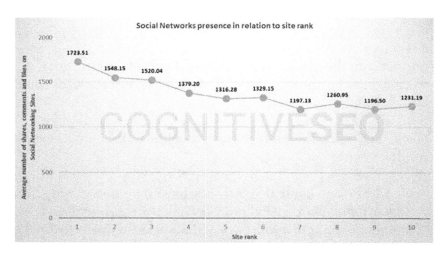

Interactions in RRSS -vs- Position of websites in Google.

And on the other hand, the Searchmetrics report on positioning factors is also clear. There is a positive correlation between social signals and position in Google.

This correlation may not be causal. This means that social networks give visibility to a web page, which generates more links to it, and therefore improves its ranking.

116

And in practice, what can we do?

First of all, it is necessary to optimize our profiles on social networks. We need to ensure that we project a consistent image across different networks, with relevant descriptions and links.

We must also get a large number of followers to extend the reach, and publish with high frequency, adapted to each social network.

It will help us to use headlines with the potential to go viral, as well as videos and images.

Buzzsumo can tell us what has worked for our competitors, what has generated more interaction.

Hashtags

People often ask if hashtags help improve results on Google.

The answer is yes. Why? Because hashtags are equivalent to keywords. They help you organize content and help users find your content. Of course, the use of hashtags varies from network to network. For example, on Instagram, they're everywhere.

Tip: Optimize your website for social networking.

Create quality, easily shared content and optimize keywords, headlines, images, videos, text and calls to action. Of course, it is convenient to add the social network buttons to the content, because they make interaction easier. As we know, videos can be inserted in the Google homepage, if they have enough relevance.

In summary:

• Name and connect your content with influencers.
• Respond to reviews, comments or other interaction.

- Participate in conversations.
- Publish frequently, as we have already said this is key.

Social networks

If we talk about each of the social networks, which are the most important for Google?

Twitter

The first social network to consider should be Twitter. Google considers links from a tweet on Twitter as a social signal. Google said in an article - http://searchengineland.com/what-social-signals-do-google-bing-really-count-55389 - that it takes into account links from Twitter - they are still links. However, it has made it clear that it also takes into account the authority of the tweeter, in some cases. The criteria for measuring that authority are:

- The number of relevant followers
- Authority of relevant followers
- The number of times that tweet has been repressed
- Number of relevant lists in which the user appears
- Number of mentions
- Ratio of followers/followers on Twitter

What is the real importance of Twitter?

Back in February 2011, a tweet from SmashingMagazine linked to the SEO guide -search engine optimization- from SEOmoz, a company specialized in search engine positioning. A week later they realized that the website where the guide is hosted reached the fourth position for the "beginner's guide" search in Google in English. Although we'll never know how many links outside of Twitter he managed to give that page the tweet. That is, we don't know if the impact was direct or indirect, but it did happen. There are other examples.

In addition, at the time of writing this book, Google re-inserts on the first page of some keywords the most recent tweets, for example, of famous politicians when you search for them. This was already the case in the past and it was changed, but it shows the good relations that exist between both companies.

Facebook

In principle, Facebook could have the same importance as Twitter for Google results, and yet it does not.
The problem is that, unlike Twitter, whose tweets are accessible, Facebook allows users levels of privacy that hide a large amount of data from Google. To obtain that data, the search engine should have a special agreement with Facebook, like the one with Microsoft's rival search engine, Bing. But since Google and Facebook don't get along, Google doesn't have access to most of Facebook's data. This could change in the future, but it is currently the case. For the time being, Facebook's direct impact on Google's results is limited. However, Facebook still plays an important, albeit indirect, role, as it serves to generate traffic and links to your website, and to promote your content.

Google +

It's a shame that Google has let its social network, Google +, die in what is one of the few failures of the company. Why? Because one of the secrets of search engine positioning was that Google+ worked very well to improve search results.

Google logically had full access to data from Google+, its social network launched in 2011 to compete with Facebook. As with Twitter, Google took into account not only the links that came from its own social network, but also a number of "signals", such as the +1 (the equivalent of "like" on facebook), or comments. And we can think that it also took into account the authority of the person recommending a link - what is his influence, how many recommendations he makes, how many friends he has, etc.

It is also possible that Google took into account the time the link is generated, the geographical location of the person generating the link, and the text next to the link.

Sparks was a Google+ utility that offered users content according to their interests. It is similar to the famous Google Alerts, since it allows users to see the latest news on a specific topic. It is not known how Google chooses the content it displays in Sparks, but we can deduce that this content undoubtedly has an additional strength in the search results.

On the other hand, it is quite possible that Google used the +1s of Google+ as a classification signal. Google gave a little push in its results to web pages that have received +1s, i.e. user recommendations.

YouTube

Another important social network for Google is YouTube - by the way, owned by Google itself. In this case we are dealing with three dimensions. On the one hand, on YouTube we can generate links to our pages. On the other hand, we can think that the presence on YouTube sends out a social signal. Finally, if we manage to optimize a video on YouTube, we can sometimes get Google to insert it on its first page of results. Let's remember that with the universal search, it inserts since 2007 videos, images and news in the results of Google's web pages.

And how can we optimize a video on YouTube? We must take into account the title of the video, the description, the file, the links it receives, the name of the file and also the number of visits that video receives, something that makes it difficult to position videos.

Instagram

This social network has grown enormously in recent years, especially in sectors such as fashion, and must also be incorporated into the general strategy of search engine positioning, although the number of links that can be generated from it is limited. But as with Facebook, it can have very beneficial indirect effects for search engine optimisation.

The practical recommendation that can be deduced from the importance of networks such as Twitter, Facebook, Instagram or YouTube, as we have already seen, is, among other things, that we should place an application on our web pages that links to both social networks, and facilitates interaction.

Tip 17
Maximize your Rankbrain (user experience)

In October 2015, Google announced in the media that it had launched a new artificial intelligence program, called "RankBrain". Specifically, it said:

> *"Over the past few months, an artificial intelligence system, called RankBrain, has interpreted a large portion of the millions of searches per second that people search for on the company's search engine"*

Even then it was known that Google was increasingly taking into account various factors related to usability and user behaviour. This news, however, was a step forward.

In case it wasn't clear, in September 2017, Nick Frost, head of Google Brain in Canada, acknowledged in a conference that several factors from RankBrain were incorporated into the algorithm.

In addition to social networks, Google obtains signals by measuring user behavior patterns on the Internet, which provide it with valuable information. For example, the exit rate -bounce rate- measures the percentage of visitors to a web page who leave after entering it without browsing the rest of the pages of that website.

If two web pages that are tied for a particular keyword show a large difference in the exit rate, Google will rank the page with the lowest exit rate because it shows that it is more useful to users. The same is true for browsing time.

The advantage of these usage signals is that they are emitted by all users, so Google has a large amount of information at its disposal.

For example, if a user wants to buy flowers, searches for "flowers for Valentine's Day", enters a website, browses for 10 minutes, and buys, that user has had a positive experience. If the same user has entered another search result before, and only lasted 3 seconds on that other web page, everything indicates that it was not what they were looking for. Google rewards the first case in its search results.

How does Google get user behavior data?

The search engine obtains data through the many sources available to it:

- Search results. For example, if a user clicks on the second result instead of the first one, for a specific search, it can be a sign that for that search the second web page is more useful than the first one.
- Google Chrome. The Google browser has a growing market share. Through Chrome, Google obtains a large amount of detailed navigation data.
- Advertising. Both Adwords and Adsense inform Google of some browsing data.
- Android. Google's Android system has a mobile market share of over 50% in many countries. In Spain it is much higher. Google therefore obtains navigation data from mobile users.
- Google applications. Programs such as Google Docs and similar provide Google with aggregated data.
- Google Analytics: There are a large number of websites that have the Google Analytics tool installed, which is very useful for users - and also for Google - when receiving aggregated data.
- Google Reader. One of the most popular RSS systems on the market, it allows Google to collect user data.

As we can see, Google has its own sources of information.

And, as if all this were not enough, Google has sometimes used data from other sources. In July 2012, Google and the US Federal Trade Commission (FTC) agreed that the search engine company would pay a fine of 22.5 million dollars (17.6 million euros) to close a case of improper processing of browsing data. It all started when Stanford Research Systems researcher Jonathan Mayer discovered Google programming code that spied on users of Apple's search engine, Safari. The spyware allows monitoring of user activities, so that it could get useful data for sending advertisements. Google claimed at the time that it was using a well-known Safari feature but always "with the consent of the users" and that the "cookies" "do not collect personal information". The judge and the FTC made it clear that Google and the other advertising companies had improperly invaded the privacy of millions of users of Apple's Safari browser through this programming code. In doing so, Google and other advertising companies were following the web surfing habits of Safari users to send them advertisements. Four months later, in November, judge Susan Illston upheld the fine, in an appeal by a consumer rights group, Consumer Watchdog, which wanted to increase the amount of the fine because it considered that the financial penalty should be "much more severe", since according to them the sum of 22.5 million is "small change" for Google. Now that we know that Google processes a large amount of information, what are the most important navigation signals from users for the search engine?

Device adaptation

When a user searches for a keyword from their mobile phone or tablet, Google rewards the web pages that are adapted to that device, and punishes those that are not. As the number of searches made from mobile phones increases - globally they are already more than 50% - it is clear that this factor becomes more important. The successive changes in the algorithm give more importance to this criterion. We must ensure that our website is optimized for all devices, especially for mobile.

Click-through rate

Called CTR - click through rate - the click through rate measures the percentage of users who enter a given web page, of all those who view it. A high click through rate is a positive indicator for Google. To achieve it, it is important that the meta description tag is attractive, and that the tag title corresponds to the user's search intention.

Bounce rate

The exit rate indicates the percentage of users who leave a website after visiting the page they entered. They do not browse the rest of the pages. A high exit rate is an indicator of poor-quality search results. To achieve a low exit rate, you must have quality content, as well as internal links to other pages of interest to the user.

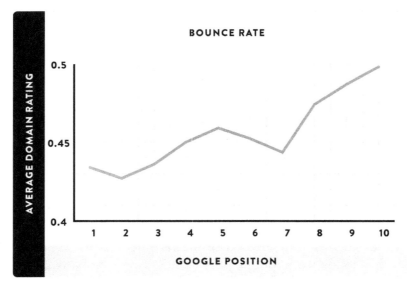

Bounce rate -vs- Position in Google

Dwell time

Google measures the time users spend on a web page. The more, the better. On the contrary, a very short navigation sends a negative signal to the search engine. It is necessary that the page interests the user, through quality content. There are data that indicate that users spend about 3 minutes on the pages that appear in the first results.

Visited pages

The more pages the user visits, the more they interact. It is convenient to have internal links to interesting pages for the user.

Return rate

If a high percentage of users return to a web page, Google perceives this as a positive thing. It is also an indicator of quality, which will improve if quality increases.

Page marked as favorite

If a considerable number of users have a website as a favourite it is a positive marker for Google.
The page is the home page in browser
It is another positive sign, that many users choose a website as their home page.

Preview / visits

Google allows users to view a web page from its search results without leaving the search results. This is called previewing. If a high percentage of users who see a page later click on it, they send a positive signal. The opposite sends a negative signal - they have seen it before and did not want to enter.

Website blocking in Chrome

In February 2011, Google launched an extension to its Chrome browser that allows users to block websites. This logically sends a negative signal to all pages on those websites.

Page load speed

Google considers the speed of a web page as a positioning factor at least since April 2010 - when it announced it in public. Probably since before, although it seems to affect especially -for the worse, of course- pages that are very slow -around 1% of the total. With each update of the algorithm, Google is giving it more importance. This criterion especially affects web pages that are slow from a search using a mobile device, penalizing them. To achieve high speed, you must have a clean code, without the page weighing more than the account, and host it on a server with sufficient capacity.

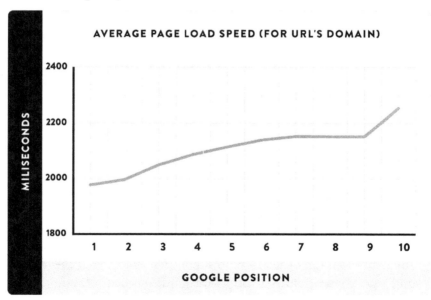

Load speed -vs- Position in Google
Study realized by Backlinko in 2016

Ending the search on a page

Google can tell if you are satisfied with your visit to a page and have completed your search, which is a positive sign, or if you have visited other pages in the same search results.

It follows that, as part of a good SEO strategy -search engine optimization- we must also optimize the user experience. If users frequently visit our websites, spend a lot of time on them, interact with them, return to them, choose them as favourites, homepages, etc. then all of this will have a positive impact on their positions on Google's result pages. And on the contrary.The reverse is also possible.

And the key to achieve all this, is to offer in our website to the user quality content, related to what you are looking for. If this is not clear, some research and surveys can help us.

• We must invest in quality content. A low-quality content, will be quickly penalized by Google through all these factors. Write the texts well, without typos, with clear phrases, so that they are understandable and appeal to the target audience of the search. Include interesting photos or videos.

• Avoid broken internal or external links, or other navigation errors.

• An additional tip is to avoid intrusive (pop-up) pages that jump or ads that do not allow the text to be read correctly. They make users angry and harm the RankBrain. They are still used more than they should be.

• And in any case, we must remember that we should never try to deceive users, since this is a bad strategy in the medium and long term.

It is logical to think that these factors linked to RankBrain affect more the pages that are on the first page of results, since Google has much more data on them. In other words, optimizing these factors is necessary to be in the first position, but by themselves they do not guarantee to get to the first page.

Tip 18
Structure your data (schema)

In view of the proliferation of information in Google, in recent years there has been a need to structure this huge amount of data. To do this, "structured data" has been created, which tells Google what kind of data it is. And it allows you to show it in your search results.

Although there are different technologies, the main search engines decided to standardize this data through schema.org, which uses Microdata.

What data are we talking about?

Google allows you to structure the following data:

- People
- Reviews
- Products
- Recipies

- Events
- Video Content
- Organizations and companies

For example, a law firm's data is represented in the:

```
<h1> Dempsey Lawyers in New York </h1>
<p> Lawyers specialized in intellectual property. </p>
<p> 7334 E. Fairway Street </p>
<p> New York, 10954, USA </p>
<p> Phone 626XXX8327 </p>
```

If the code uses the Microdata format it would be:

```
<div itemscope itemtype="http://schema.org/LocalBusiness">
<h1><span itemprop="name"> Dempsey Lawyers in New York </span></h1>
```

```
<span  itemprop="description">  Lawyers  specialized  in
intellectual property. </span>
<div   itemprop="address"   itemscope   itemtype="http://
schema.org/PostalAddress">
<span itemprop="streetAddress"> 7334 E. Fairway Street </
span>
<span itemprop="addressLocality"> New York, 10954</span>
,
<span itemprop="addressRegion">USA</span>
</div>
Phone: <span itemprop="telephone">626XXX8327</span>
</div>
```

This allows Google to understand what the data is, and to manage it as such.

Does this affect Google positioning?

In Juan Prieto's TFM paper, mentioned above, we can see that 36% of the websites in first position for competitive keywords in the toy sector are already using it. If we remove the Amazon web pages from these results, which do not use it at the moment, we see that this percentage rises to 69%.

It is not one of the most important factors, but as with other data, it does not harm to use it, since it will help to increase the click rate (CTR) in some cases, which is a positive sign, that improves RankBrain, as we have seen before.

In Summary

How must be a winning webpage
in Google?

Once we have analyzed the main factors of positioning in Google, we will summarize how a web page that aspires to achieve good results for a specific keyword should be.

The most important are summarized in these seven points:

1) You should include the keyword in the tag title, meta description tag, alt tag, the url and H1 header (unique).

2) It should have a considerable length of original text, at least 200 words or more, with an appropriate keyword density, generally between 2% and 3%, although this will depend on the sector. It should also have some outgoing links to reliable pages.

3) It should have a high Pagerank. And it should have a large number of inbound links to that page, from relevant pages, with anchor text related to the keyword but varied, and following a natural pattern.

4) It should be hosted on a website that in turn receives a large number of inbound links, is old and has a large number of pages indexed in Google.

5) It will help if, under certain circumstances, your domain name matches or contains the keyword exactly.

6) You should have interaction on social networks, the more the better, especially on Twitter and Youtube but also on Facebook or Instagram.

7) It should have a high RankBrain, and for this purpose, quality content, high loading speed, be adapted to all devices, etc.

Extra Tip

Avoid Google's penalties

There is a branch of search engine optimization called "Black Hat SEO". It is the black magic of the industry.

"Unscrupulous wizards" who are not afraid to use any method to achieve their ends.

It is called that way because the bad guys in the cowboy movies usually wear a black hat, while the good guys wear "white hats" that is, they are the ones who practice "White Hat SEO" the good SEO.

Of course, there is also a gray area, which is where the "Grey Hat" SEOs live. This looks like a hat shop. Grey hats are the ones on the border, in an area where it is not clear if what they do is appropriate or may violate some Google rule.

Well. Actually, black SEO usually ends up badly, just like in Western movies, the bad guy, Google, ends up blowing his brains out.

A few days ago, just before writing these lines, we interviewed a young man for a Top Position SEO job. He came from an agency where they practice this "black magic". He told us that over and over again, the results ended up being bad, and that the clients, for the most part, ended up leaving.

The "black" shortcuts in search engine positioning are expensive, because Google ends up catching you.

And then the penalties come.

When in doubt as to whether something is right or wrong, put yourself in the shoes of a Google expert who is checking it out. Will he or she find it right, wrong or regular?

You should know that Google has two types of penalties. The

algorithmic ones and the manual ones.

In the former, it's a robot that shoots you. It happens when there is a change in the algorithm, or when the Google robot detects some inappropriate behaviour.

In the latter, it's a person who shoots you.

How do we know if Google has penalized us? In the case of manual penalties, we'll see it in our Search Console. There is a specific section called "manual actions" within "search traffic". There we see if we have any manual penalties.

In the case of automatic penalties, we will have to analyze some relevant metrics -of organic traffic for example- to realize.

Penalties may be specific, in which case they affect the results of a single keyword or set of keywords, or they may be generic, in which case they affect the entire website.

The most serious generic penalty is to 'de-index' an entire website from the Google index. This means, no more and no less, that the website ceases to exist for the search engine. It does not appear in any results. It is the "civil death" of a website, and logically has very serious consequences. It has happened to important websites, such as, for example, when the BMW website in Germany (https://www.theregister.co.uk/2006/02/06/bmw_removed/) was "excommunicated" for a time for carrying out "cloaking" practices - which consists of showing specific, over-optimised pages to the search engine that the user does not see.

What does Google penalize? The list of inappropriate behaviors is long, but the practices that cause the most relevant penalties are, besides the mentioned cloaking:

- Domain registered by a spammer. Google will penalize

a website whose domain is owned by a person who has previously been penalized.

• Of course, pages with misleading redirects or malicious behavior, such as pages that impersonate or install viruses, Trojans or other malicious programs.

• Keyword stuffing. In Google's early days, it was common to put the keyword of interest everywhere, artificially increasing the density of the keyword. If the text is hidden or disguised, it is even more serious. It has not worked for a long time, and this practice generates an automatic penalty by Google. To avoid it, you have to write naturally, for humans, not for search engine robots.

• Copied, automatically generated or poor quality content. Copying is automatically detected, and at least disidexes the page in question - Google does not want multiple identical contents to appear in its search results. Poor quality content may be detected by a search engine employee, in which case he or she may unindex a page. If it is widespread, it will greatly affect the website as a whole. We must therefore, once again, generate quality content.

• Outgoing links from a hidden page, or to pages of bad reputation. This is the Badrank we have explained before. It detects it automatically.

• Unnatural outgoing links. That is, if a Google employee thinks you've sold links.

• Unnatural inbound links, not relevant, massive, not varied in pagerank or the same type. Google will think that you have bought them. We have already explained that inbound links must be natural, with natural growth, varied, with pageranks distributed heterogeneously. Google penalizes participating in what it calls "link schemes" that links generated from poor quality websites, created for this sole purpose.

• A large number of links with identical anchor text. As we have explained, anchor texts must follow natural patterns.

• The abuse of enriched fragments, i.e. structured data.

To prevent all these penalties we must follow Google's guidelines [9] and generate quality content that is naturally linked .

[9] https://support.google.com/webmasters/answer/35769?hl=es-419

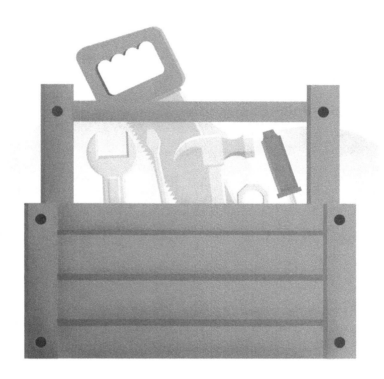

SEO Tools

There are a lot of tools that can help you manage your Google positioning. I have made a selection of the most relevant.

SEOQuake.

http://www.seoquake.com/

SEOQuake installs a bar that offers a large number of free metrics, and works in virtually all browsers.

Google tool for keywords

http://www.google.com/intl/en/adwords/

We've already talked about it, it's free, it's not very accurate, but it gives you an idea of the volume of searches for a keyword.

Google Trends.

https://trends.google.com/trends/?geo=US

We've talked about her too. It's free, although it's not very accurate either. It allows you to see the evolution of the volume of searches.

Google Page Speed Insights.

https://developers.google.com/speed/pagespeed/insights

Another free tool from Google, which tells you the speed of your website on all different devices.

**Google Search Console
(before was Webmasters Tools)**

https://search.google.com/search-console/about

Again, a free tool from Google to help you manage your relationship with Google. You can detect and correct problems with indexing, sitemap, penalties. Etc.

Google Analytics

https://analytics.google.com

It is not the object of this book, but this free Google tool will allow you to know, among many other things, some data about organic traffic, keywords that generate it, etc. We know that in these matters it is inaccurate, and in some aspects even opaque.

Ubersuggest

http://ubersuggest.org/

Useful for detecting long tail keywords.

Redirect Checker.

http://www.redirect-checker.org/

Lets you know if you've done the redirects correctly.

Schema Creator

http://www.schema-creator.org/

It's free and allows you to automatically generate schema.org.

SEO Browser

http://seo-browser.com

Lets you see a web page as a search engine robot sees it.

Semrush

https://semrush.com

Free and paid version. It allows you to analyze a large number of metrics related to links, keywords and results. It is certainly the market leader.

Moz

http://moz.com/tools

It has a free version and other paid versions. A reference in the world of search engine positioning.

Ahrefs

https://ahrefs.com

Recognized tool to analyze organic traffic volume, keywords, competitors and opportunities

Majestic

https://majestic.com

Free and paid version. It is a powerful tool for analyzing links, keywords and search results. It also allows you to see the level of competence of specific keywords.

These last five tools have paid versions that offer all the functionalities, and they largely overlap each other, so you don't need all of them, but in most cases one of them will be enough.

Final Reflection

As a gift, a final reflection

The Google effect: consequences of its operation for participation and democracy on the Internet

We already have a good idea of how Google works. As a gift, I leave you with a chapter on the implications of how it works for the ongoing debates on the Internet, participation and democracy.

When we talk about concepts such as digital democracy, society 2.0, or cyberactivism, we often discuss whether the Internet really strengthens participation, redistributes power in favor of citizens, and allows for a deepening of democracy, or the opposite.

Within this context, once we have unravelled how Google classifies the different web pages according to each specific search, a fascinating debate opens up before us.

Do Google's results promote citizen participation and democracy?

Or, on the contrary, do they reinforce the existing large centres of power?

Let us recall that in 2005, Joe Trippi, an American political leader, responsible for the success of his then candidate Howard Dean on the Internet, said that "the Internet is the most democratizing innovation we have ever seen, above even the printing press" - narrated on page 235 of his book "The revolution will not be televised: democracy, the Internet and the overthrow of everything".

Several authors, including Trippi himself, have been quick to link the Internet with the citizens' movements that in 2011 overthrew the dictatorial regimes of Tunisia, Egypt and Libya, provoked the resignation of the prime minister of Yemen and shook up the regimes of Syria and many other Arab countries. In this case, the most immediate association has been with social networks, to which the most direct link to these citizen movements is attributed.

Similarly, the origins of the M-15 movement in Spain, and its emulations in many other countries, seem closely linked to the Internet. This is the opinion of numerous experts such as Ismael Peña, who was interviewed on this subject and who does not hesitate to argue that the movement would not have existed without social networks or some of the organizers of the 15M in Seville, who state that "15M was born on the net and will always remain there". [10]

The same opinion is held and categorically affirmed by the Internet media researcher, Eva María Ferreras Rodríguez in the conclusions of her article on 15M and Twitter: "we can say that the 15-M movement was born and developed on the Internet, therefore it can be taken as a sample of cyberactivism" (Ferreras, 2011, El Movimiento 15-M y su evolución en Twitter, Cuadernos de Comunicación e Innovación Telos, number 89, available at http://sociedadinformacion. fundacion.telefonica.com/seccion=1266&idioma=es_ES&id=2011102410330001&activo=6.do#)

Therefore, there is a consensus in attributing to some parts of the Internet, especially to social networks, some or a lot of importance in citizen movements.

Regardless of whether this role attributed to social networks is real or exaggerated, we must ask ourselves, what role do the search engines play, specifically Google, which is the hegemonic one?

On the optimists' side, an author like Steven Johnson vehemently defended in his work Emergence, the connected lives of ants,

---

[10] https://www.publico.es/espana/movimiento-15m-nacio-red-y.html

brains, cities and software (2002) that the Internet, and the search engines, function according to the process that he calls "emergence". In his words: "like the dialectical logic of the nineteenth century, the emergent vision of the world belongs to our time, shaping our habits and perception of it".

This emergent dynamic, applied to the Internet, means that: "the role of the Internet in all this will not have to do with its ability to distribute high-quality video images or spectacular sounds. Instead, the Internet will provide the meta-data that allows these structures to organize themselves. It will be the central repository and marketplace for all our mediated patterns of behavior. And those patterns, instead of being restricted to Madison Avenue and TRW, will be available to consumers, who will be able to create community maps of all the data and entertainment available on the Internet.

This "émergence", is a decentralized system, operating from the bottom up. In this sense, Google, according to Johnson, is limited to allowing the opinions and decisions of the users to emerge, who are the ones who link, and the most important part of the system, in the same way that ants are in a colony, while the search engine acts as a "queen ant", who according to Johnson has a secondary role - as he explains in his chapter "the myth of the queen ant".

Others are not so optimistic. In Matthew Hindman's opinion, in his book The Myth of Digital Democracy, 2009, in order to understand the weight of the different actors on the Internet, it is necessary to analyse their link structure or hyperlinks. This structure follows exponential statistical laws, which tend to concentration, so that a few websites end up monopolizing the vast majority of links and traffic. This tendency, moreover, reinforces itself, in a virtuous - or vicious, depending on whether we think the process is positive or negative- circle. In this context, search engines in general, and Google in particular, would be reinforcing this trend.

Even before Hindman, Lessing had postulated, in his work The Future of Ideas, 2001, that the Internet is made up of three layers, and that its architecture is changeable, so efforts by commercial interests or power to change it could alter its open nature.

And both Barabási and Albert, in their book Emergence of Scaling in Random Network (1999) and Kumar in Trawling the Web for Emerging Cyber-Communities, (1999), warn that the distribution of links on the Internet is not equal, far from it, but is concentrated in a way that is similar or even superior to people's wealth, in the same way that other previous authors had shown that this concentration occurs in fields as diverse as business size, economics (Krugman in Complex Landscapes in Economic Geography, 1994) or the number of sexual contacts (Liljeros in The Web of Human Sexual Contacts, 2001).

The reality is that a few huge websites receive a high number of links. Hindman argues that this distribution affects Google search results as well as traffic. In his own words, "In these study data, the number of links a website receives and the visits to that website have a high correlation of 0.704 (the maximum would be 1)". Therefore, the number of links going to a website may precede its traffic volume.

Hindman and his collaborators don't just stand there. They develop the theory they call "Googlyarchy". This theory argues that "the number of links to a website is the most important part of determining its visibility on the Internet. The websites that receive the most links receive, ceteris paribus, the most traffic. Secondly, we can conclude that the domain of a niche or segment is a general law of the Internet. In each group or theme of the Internet, there is a website that receives the most links and traffic. Finally, this Googlery, "feeds itself, so that it is reinforced and perpetuated in time"

In other words, the links are concentrated on the Internet, making the websites that receive the most links dominate the search results, getting more visibility and more links. In that context, Google would reinforce the dominance of the most powerful websites, since it gives visibility to the pages and websites that have received the most links.

In the same line of argument, Cho and Roy, in their work Impact of Search Engines on page Popularity (2004), had argued years earlier that search engines contributed to the concentration of traffic and power on a few websites.
In contrast to these theories, an author such as Fortunato in The Egalitarian Effect of Search Engines (2006) - the egalitarian effect of search engines - postulates exactly the opposite. According to Fortunato, search engines help to alleviate the inequalities of the Internet, disperse traffic and make it less concentrated than it would be without search engines.

Another author on the critical side is Alexander Havalais, who in his book Search Engine Society (2009) argues that search engines create winners and losers on the Internet, increase inequality and concentrate power. In his words "search result rankings exist, because there is demand for them. However, such rankings inherently reflect the status quo, and they may not be in the public interest. The concept of relevance is entirely subjective."

On the other hand, Halavais is particularly concerned with the homogenizing cultural effect of American search engines such as Google, which he says tend to favor results from American websites, since they are considered more "authoritative" by the search engine. This latter criticism could theoretically be qualified because Google has cleverly developed national versions of its search engine, which promote - supposedly - national content. Furthermore, language is fundamental to Google's search results, which are in Spanish, for example, for searches in Spanish. There does seem to be a bias in favor of U.S. websites, as long as they contain pages in Spanish.

For his part, the author Gideon Haigh argues in his essay Information idol, how Google is making us stupid (2006), that Google is then comfortable, generating complacency, by giving us an easy and fast service, on which we can depend.

The debate is intense and exciting: Is the system built by Google one of the "authoritarian techniques" defined by Lewis Mumford in 1964? Or, on the contrary, is the hegemonic search engine a force that democratizes the Internet, increasing the number of "people with a voice?

Selection, filters and information

The concept of "Gatekeeper" comes from the Field Theory of Social Psychology developed by Kurt Lewin in his studies of the 1940s on the interactive dynamics of social groups. The General Information Theory (GIT) has given this concept its own profile.

Lewin argued that, in the informational process or sequence of information through the communicative channels in a group, the lapse or blockage of unity through the channel depends largely on what happens in the filter area.

Filter zones are controlled by objective rule systems or by "gatekeepers" who have the power to decide whether to let information through or not.

These theories have been applied to the selection of press releases - most agency releases are deleted - among other fields. Renowned experts in information theory, such as Professor Felicísimo Valbuena de la Fuente, have analyzed the concept and its application to General Information Theory.

Quoting Professor Valbuena, in his work General Information Theory: "The power to "bring together or separate", the more specifically human power, takes in TGI the form of "giving coverage or not giving coverage".

Well, at the dawn of the 21st century, we can assume that Google, both in its general search engine for web pages and in its specific search engine for news - Google News - acts as a "gatekeeper" of information. A systemic "gatekeeper", which strictly complies -robotically- with the rules of its own algorithm.

And in the light of this research, we can deduce some of these rules and what they imply for participation and democracy.

Various studies and experience show us that at least some of the rules of Google's systemic filtering may not necessarily favour participation or democracy, and at worst they may even encourage the status quo and established powers.

Let's look at some of the criteria we have verified throughout the book.

Website age

As we have seen, the average age of the websites hosting the winning pages is very high for competitive search terms.

We can say, strictly speaking, that Google tends towards "gerontocracy". Its algorithm has a systemic bias in favour of old structures, as it rewards the web pages of older websites. It follows, therefore, that it penalizes web pages hosted on recent websites, and therefore penalizes these as well.

Google's filter therefore penalises those portals or websites that are not very old. As we have seen, this characteristic is related to the fact that the "bad guys" who try to abuse the search engines -called "spammers"- create new websites permanently, and therefore Google is partly right to distrust them, but this does not mean that this criterion does not have a potential negative impact on democracy or participation.

Applied to the commercial world, this means that a new, innovative travel service company, for example, is at a disadvantage in Google compared to established travel companies with older websites. Applied to political campaigns, for example, it could mean that a new political party with a recent website would be at a disadvantage in terms of appearing in search results on political or electoral issues.

Another potential consequence of such a criterion is that it favors those who can buy old domains - as these are bought and sold. Thus, there is another economic bias, which allows the wealthy to have an advantage in Google when acquiring an old domain. Applied to Google News, this means that Google's news filter favors established media -which have old websites- and penalizes new ones -which have recent websites.

On the other hand, as we have already seen, we may think that this criterion favours websites from the United States, a country where the Internet was developed before - many of the old websites are American - while it disadvantages, for example, French websites - a country where the Internet was imposed late, after winning over other similar indigenous technologies.

Pages indexed to the entire website

Similarly, Google rewards pages hosted on large websites, which have a high number of indexed pages. This criterion also has its logic, but like the previous one, it is doubtful that it promotes participation or greater democracy. A company, institution or government will have the resources to develop a large number of pages that can be indexed on Google. On the contrary, an emerging association or group will have much more difficulty in generating content and indexing a large number of pages.

Inbound links to the entire website

Another confirmed criterion is the number of inbound links to the entire website.

Like the previous ones, the dominant groups -of whatever nature- that manage to generate and index a large number of pages, will have an advantage when it comes to achieving a large number of links to the website as a whole because, as it is easy to deduce, the more pages we have, the more total links we will obtain.

In addition, those with the economic resources to do so will be able to acquire links in a marketplace that, although penalized by Google, exists in various variants.

We see therefore that, although Google has never officially recognised the importance of the website where a web page is hosted -it says it classifies individual web pages- this is revealed as fundamental in at least three of the most important criteria. Moreover, we have to consider that these criteria are on the increase. The advantage they generate is growing every day - the large websites that dominate the Internet are getting older every day, receiving more links and containing more pages.

A priori, this does not encourage participation or democracy. Quite the opposite, perhaps. However, it is fair to bring up a possible exception: Wikipedia.

It is striking how many "winning" web pages belong to Wikipedia. Often, Wikipedia web pages achieve top positions when the keyword is a common or proper name - countries, cities, celebrities. We have already seen why Google likes Wikipedia so much. It is due to the enormous number of pages indexed and the huge number of incoming links to the website in general, as well as the advanced age of the website - the general website, Wikipedia.org is over 18 years old. For all these reasons, being hosted on Wikipedia gives any web page a great advantage. In addition, Wikipedia's web pages adapt their title tag to each definition, have a high number of internal and outgoing links. These Wikipedia hosted web pages usually receive a high number of inbound links themselves.

A priori, Wikipedia is a participatory website, where different people contribute and write new articles or edit existing ones. This is positive and reinforces the thesis of an open and participatory Internet. However, it must be qualified, since the final word on the modifications that a private individual can make to the entries on Wikipedia is held by a select number of editors - the wikipedians - who are not necessarily objective, but flesh and blood people, who have and assert their opinions - for example political. It is logical to think that the people who are most interested in writing, commenting on and moderating political articles have their own opinions and biases in this respect, and criticism abounds, for example in the United States, which claims that Wikipedia has a bias towards the left in politics.

On the other hand, what would happen if a media outlet or a person bought Wikipedia, something that is theoretically possible?

Inbound links to the webpage

In contrast to these three structural criteria, which concern the website as a whole, and which, as we have seen, favour a priori large and resourced websites, there is one criterion that could, at least in theory, increase democracy and participation in search results. This is the number of inbound links received by the individual webpage. In effect, this criterion would allow a large number of "players" on the Internet to link to a page, and through all these "votes" elevate the web page to the heights of Google. That way, theoretically -let's remember that this was the origin of Google's algorithm- a publicly acclaimed web page could emerge or stand out.

Here we can find an insterstice, a democratic and participatory gap that justifies the optimism of many experts or supposed experts. The more weight this criterion has, the more valid Johnson's concept of "emergence" or "emergence", discussed above, will be.

However, we observe that this criterion is losing weight, while structural factors are gaining it. It seems that more and more, Google structurally chooses - through general website criteria - which are the winning web pages. Caution is in order.

Finally, there is another factor that affects Google's results. This is the services of consultancy firms that specialise in improving positions. Google insists on saying that they do not affect its search results in any way. We know that, once again, the search engine is not telling the whole truth.

www.ingramcontent.com/pod-product-compliance
Lightning Source LLC
LaVergne TN
LVHW022124060326
832903LV00063B/3690